My

Naked

Soul

by Savon Lindsay

'Click... click... click!' Suddenly, it was the scary, distinctive sound of a hand gun. But for some reason the gun wasn't blowing the top of my head off. One of Reggie's brothers was pulling the trigger and every time the gun clicked, my body flinched because I thought I had been shot. My hands were going crazy trying to feel a bullet wound, but there was none... no blood... no anything. But this dude was still pulling the trigger.

A divine intervention had taken place that night... I truly believe to this day that God had spared my life because that same gun would kill a friend of mine a month later... when I realized the gun was not firing, I made my break for the door and ran like lightening had struck me dead in the ass. I don't think I've ever ran that fast in my entire life.

As I fled down the hallway, the only thing I could see were the street lights at the end of the hall. When I made it to the curb where my car was parked, I heard a loud booming noise and looking back just for a second, I could see Lawrence had some how managed to grab the shotgun. While he and Reggie were struggling, the gun went off. The blast of the shotgun had tore a hole in the roof of the Ed's Hotel instead of the back of my head.

When I reached the middle of Cottonwood road, I felt a heavy blow upside the back of my head. Once again, Reggie was beaming down on me. He had hit me with the barrel of the shotgun, and my legs fell from under me. Looking up from the ground, I was facing 'THE FAT LADY. 'She looked like a vicious, twisted mask, and an enraged black face with a double barrel shotgun. As I looked right in the eye of this Lady of Death, I screamed, please, please! Don't kill me! Don't kill me like this! Please don't kill me!

For just a moment my whole life flashed before my eyes. I had heard somewhere before that when a person was about to die, there life would flash before them. Fortunately for me, the Fat

Lady didn't sing that night, but it was the voice of racing police cars and sirens on an ambulance.

After that, I didn't remember too much, but I remember my body felt real cold, as if it had been placed in a tomb. When I looked up, there was a man dressed in a white uniform. I thought, 'had I actually died, but just didn't know it? I asked myself over and over again, 'Was I actually dead? Was I to die like this, like an animal in the street! Caught up in this rat hole a horrible dope fiend's death, with a spike in my arm and a pipe in my mouth. Was a bag of dope worth this? Wasn't my life worth more then that...? Damn, damn, damn! I said repeatedly. This is got to be the coldest way in the world for me to die.

When I came to my senses, I realized that the man in the white uniform was an attendant at the Kern County Morgue. Yes! The County morgue was where my addition had taken me... then my poor mother was called down to the morgue to identify her son.

Well, I guess it wasn't time for the miracle of change in my life that night... you would think that would be enough for any fool to realize there was something incredibly wrong, after I had been beaten, shot at, and declared dead from an overdose.

You have to understand the overwhelming power and insanity of the disease of addition to know all these horrible, life-threatening events that took place that night... I just couldn't stop the obsession to use... this vicious cycle, this insidious predator had taken over my mind, body and soul. The only thing on my mind... after my eyes opened and I realize I wasn't going to die... was where in the world I could find me a bag of dope that time of night. Where could I find me another blast, another crack puff...another... damn drug.

ISBN: 1-4033-7799-5 (e-book)
ISBN: 1-4033-7800-2 (Paperback)

This book is printed on acid free paper.

Special Assistant: Robert Sollars

1stBooks – rev. 6/23/02

Acclaim for Savon Lindsay's
My Naked Soul

"Powerful and relentlessly real."
> —Eldridge Cleaver, author of national bestseller, *Soul on Ice*

"With searing images and a powerful voice, he is part of a new literary trend: a Black Virgil who leads his audience through the inferno of maximum security prisons, street gangs, crack houses and body bags at the morgue—to the purgatory of recovery."
> — Jason Reynolds, *Creative Factory*

"A powerful and incredible Black experience."
> — Dr. Acklyn Lynch,University of Maryland Social Science, Activist, Educator, Author of *Nightmare Overhangin Darkly*

"He sears our hearts and minds with electric-fire truth about his personal journey on the path of self-destruction, painting with words the darkened, muted colors of self-deception, degradation, and false grandeur of the drug world. He captures the powerful rhythm of the imprisonment of a "lost soul," taking us with him to the very edge of death, then leading us back, fighting for his life and recovery. Savon Lindsay is the poet of both revolution and resurrection of the human spirit."
> —Marih Alyn-Claire, Bioscience writer, Journalist

Savon Lindsay's

My Naked Soul

Also by Savon Lindsay:

The Soul of an Addict
and
Tired of Being Sick and Tired

About the author...

Savon was born in Bakersfield, California in 1950. He started writing when he was seven years old. His first piece, a poem about Louis Armstrong, won him a ribbon of achievement for best poem and recital. Drugs and crime took Savon in and out of California prisons and jails for over 30 years.

In jail, Savon studied many Black authors. His prison time became a spiritual and artistic journey because his passion for learning was so intense. Once Savon was released, he went to Compton College on a student loan and studied sociology and psychology. It was very hard because of his drug use and alcoholism, but during that time he managed to achieve another award for Black poetry. His addiction landed him in and out of prison until 1992. Then the light went on; three years later, he found recovery.

Throughout those years and throughout his addiction, Savon never relented in his desire to create. To express the pains and joys, the heartfelt sorrow, yet—always hope. A commitment undying in the life of a man. A commitment undying in the life of Savon Lindsay.

My Naked Soul

A startling autobiography of
a Black recovering addict

Savon Lindsay

Published in joint cooperation with:

We Do Recover Publications
818 SW Third Avenue, P.O. Box 1322
Portland, Oregon 97204-2405
and
The Copper Sylk Company,
Book Publishing Division,
P.O. Box 3802 Portland, Oregon 97208-3802

editing and layout by Bryan Pollard
cover photography and design by Bryan Pollard
editorial assistance by Jason Reynolds
drawings by Clifford Lewis

Contents

Part 1

Part 2

To My Grandmother

This book is dedicated solely to my
grandmother, Theresa Cooper, who passed on
March 12, 1996, but who lives and breathes
in my spirit today. She was there for me when
I couldn't be there for myself.

PART 1

Chapter 1   **From the Womb to the Tomb**

A Bottle, a bag, a rock you feast
from the womb to the tomb, in the belly of the Beast,
the County Morgue and a Life of Crime
As you **S c r e a m** for a Hit, One more time,
A Bottomless pit
trapped with scorn,
a Dopefiend Dies
but another one...was born...

There was an overcast of grayish blue skies as the moon seemed to cry out in a desperate attempt to flee the inescapable night. There was talk of rain in the small town of Bakersfield, California. But the night seemed to explode, as I found the vein I had been looking for. Heroin, China-white, that's what it was called at that time, sometime in January, 1981.

I was thirty-one years old, and a hope-to-die dopefiend. China-white had come out many years before I had tried it, but it was known to all for its pure whiteness and the overwhelming power it possessed. I had just gotten out of the Kern County jail, another jail-house, another institution, and I thought I owed it to myself to get loaded because, after all, I was a *dopefiend*. Besides, this time I thought I had the magic formula on the street game. Crack cocaine was getting popular at that time, and I was the type of addict you just couldn't miss. So there I was with a spike in my arm and a crack pipe in my mouth.

We had been up twenty-four- seven, shooting dope and smoking crack like it wasn't nobody's business. Lawrence was a very good friend of mine (wherever you are my brother, my prayers are with you). He was an addict like myself but for the life of me I could never figure out how in the world he could shoot dope all day and deal drugs at the same time. That eerie night, my friend Lawrence had passed out in bed with one of his honnies.

We were in the shooting gallery in Ed's Hotel on Cottonwood Road in Bakersfield. It was a small, unpleasant room where dopefiends congregated to do their drugs. As my blood rushed up into the syringe, I knew it was a direct hit. Releasing the tie from my arm, an old head rag I had been using for my hair, this powerful drug that had made many men slaves, had started taking its toll. Suddenly, life had become a blissful fantasy, a pleasure impossible to measure. Whatever my problems were before, they had been magically taken away. All my minds-eye could see now was an overwhelming freedom, unexplainable to anyone but myself.

When I came out of that dopefiend fog, so high I thought I had wings to fly, I remember somebody saying, "Hey, brother man, you all right." The next thing I remember was a loud crashing sound, and when I looked up, coming out of a nod, hinges were falling from the front door. Four of the baddest motherfuckers I've ever seen in my life came breaking through the door. Reggie, one of the brothers that came through the door first, was followed by his three brothers, and they were looking for yours truly, *me*. Their sister, Diane, had told them that I was the dude that burglarized her house after she had passed out that day.

I remembered taking Diane home. She was so loaded she didn't know which way was up. Since she hadn't had any money to steal, I stole anything and everything that wasn't nailed down. At the time, I thought I was within my rights to take from her. I was a self-proclaimed pimp and hustler and had the magic formula prescribed by Ice Berg Slim. Ice Berg Slim (Robert Beck) was a notorious pimp from the ol' school and had written a few books about how he pimped ho's. Every time I went to jail or the penitentiary, I'd always read his books, as well as those of Donald Goines. I'd also read other books, like Leroy Jones (Amiri Baraka), Nikki Giovanni, Malcolm X, Dick Gregory, Maya

Angelou, Gill Scott Heron, Robert Wright, and
many others, but at that time in my life, I found Ice
Berg Slim's books the most appealing. I thought if
he could master the street game on pimping, so
could I.

As I sat there almost comatose from those
deadly, powerful drugs, china-white and crack
cocaine, looking straight in the barrel of that
nigga's shotgun. My first thought was, if God
could just get me out of this one, I'd surely do the
right thing. Then, just as suddenly, the drugs started
making me feel like superman. I thought, "what
would my hero Ice Berg Slim do in a situation like
this?" So I grabbed the barrel of the gun and did
what any fool would do, I started fighting for my
natural-born, black ass.

It was like the "Thriller in Manilla" in the
dopehouse that night but the gorilla wasn't George
Foreman and I wasn't Muhammad Ali. I was
fighting for my life, not a title fight, where the
loser would go home and regroup. No! The loser
was going to pay with his life. If I didn't get out of
this, I knew in my heart of hearts, I was going to
be as dead as the graveyard. Later, I found out that

all four brothers had been smoking sherm. Sherm was commonly known as elephant tranquilizer, PCP, whack, or buck naked, and you can imagine what kind of effect it was having on these four brothers.

I remembered my Thunderbird bottle sitting next to me I had been drinking from earlier. With one hand on the barrel of the shotgun, I took the bottle in hand and laid some serious licks upside Reggie's head. "Damn!" I said to myself, "the bottle hadn't even phased this nigga." He acted as if the blows from the bottle were pure annoyance. The blows were like the irritance of a small fly that needed killing, that needed to die, and that's exactly what this nigga was trying to do. He was trying to kill me.

There I was swinging this Thunderbird bottle upside Reggie's head when, all of a sudden, he seemed to tire from that bullshit. He reached down and grabbed me by the throat and started to lift my little ass in mid-air. He threw me across the room, and I ended up beside an old refrigerator. Damn! If there wasn't another gun being pointed at me. With all the commotion that was going on, my partner

Lawrence finally came to.

Once Lawrence had got his ass up, he was holding his own pretty good. They used to say that if Lawrence hit you, you better look behind you and find out what was holding you up. Lawrence was much heavier than me, and was as wide as a brick shithouse. He hadn't been out of prison too long himself, and while there, he took up the art of weight-lifting. Like so many other blacks, Lawrence had taken advantage of the weight-yard. But I, on the other hand, was more into the books. I read almost anything and everything I could get my hands on. My belief at the time was like the ol' saying, "Pimps don't die, they multiply," and so I didn't lift anything heavier than a bankroll. I thought I didn't need to get physical because, like Ice Berg Slim, I would pimp or die.

"Click... click... click!" Suddenly, it was the scary, distinctive sound of a handgun. But for some reason the gun wasn't blowing the top of my head off. One of Reggie's brothers was pulling the trigger and every time the gun clicked, my body flinched because I thought I had been shot. My hands were going crazy trying to feel a bullet wound, but there was none... no blood... no anything. But this dude was still pulling the trigger.

A divine intervention had taken place that night. I believe that's the only way to describe what happened . The gun was a twenty-two caliber, Saturday Night Special. An old handgun someone had sold him, and fortunately for me, the firing pin wasn't working. I truly believe to this day that God had spared my life because that same gun would kill a friend of mine a month later, and Reggie's brother would face a murder-one charge. He was sentenced to a term of twenty-five years to life. Years would pass and I'd shake my head in wonder, and realize how very blessed I really was.

When I realized the gun wasn't firing, I made my break for the door and ran like lightning had struck me dead in the ass. I don't think I've ever ran that fast in my entire life.

The Ed's Hotel has since been torn down but I still remember that old dilapidated building. It's smell of piss and excrement where some ho had squat in a hurry so as not to miss her money or a winehead relieving himself, not really caring where

he slept that particular night. Each room was small
with a bed and if you were real lucky you got a
refrigerator. The bathroom and shower area were
in the dingy hallway. Most of the people who lived
there were either transient people coming through
town to work in the fields, the disabled on social
security, or welfare recipients stuck in their own
little worlds. But primarily, there were would-be
players, hustlers and dopefiends trying to catch the
impossible in a town of broken dreams. There
were wine and liquor stores directly across the
street, and all down the street were night clubs,
bars and houses of prostitution.

Cottonwood Road, also known as Lakeview or
the strip, was known all over the country for its
frequent killings and drug accessibility.
Bakersfield is located about two hundred or so
miles north of Mexico. To the south is Los Angeles
and to the north there's Fresno and the Bay Area.
So that put the city of Bakersfield just about in the
middle of all the major drug trafficking on the west
coast.

As I fled down the hallway, the only thing I
could see were the street lights at the end of the

hall. When I made it to the curb where my car was parked, I heard a loud booming noise and looking back just for a second. I could see Lawrence had somehow managed to grab the shotgun. While he and Reggie were struggling, the gun went off. The blast of the shotgun had tore a hole in the roof of Ed's Hotel instead of the back of my head. I guess the loud blast had kept the others at bay, because I didn't see any of them anymore. But my old partner Lawrence had saved the day. He had saved my ass but by the grace of God.

When my feet hit the ground, I realized one of my shoes was missing, but I didn't miss a beat because I continued to run like crazy. I passed up my car and any other car that didn't have a door open with my name on the seat.

When I reached the middle of Cottonwood Road, I felt a heavy blow upside the back of my head. Once again, Reggie was beaming down on me. He had hit me with the barrel of the shotgun and my legs fell from under me. Looking up from the ground, I was facing "The Fat Lady." She looked like a vicious, twisted mask, an enraged, black face with a double barreled shotgun. As I looked right in the eye of this "Lady of Death," I screamed, "Please, please! Don't kill me! Don't kill me like this! Please don't kill me!"

For just a moment, my whole life flashed before my eyes.

I had heard somewhere before, that when a person was about to die, there life would flash before them. Fortunately for me, "The Fat Lady" didn't sing that night, but it was the voice of racing police cars and sirens on an ambulance.

After that, I didn't remember too much, but I remember my body felt real cold, as if it had been placed in a tomb. When I looked up, there was a man dressed in a white uniform. I thought, "Had I actually died, but just didn't know it?" I asked myself over and over again, "Was I actually dead? Was I to die like this, like an animal in the street! Caught up in this rat hole, a horrible dopefiends death with a spike in my arm and a pipe in my mouth? Was a bag of dope or a rock worth this? Wasn't my life worth more than that...? Damn, damn, damn!" I said repeatedly, "This has got to be the coldest way in the world for me to die."

When I came to my senses, I realized that the

man in the white uniform was an attendant at the
Kern County Morgue. Yes, the County Morgue was
where my addiction had taken me and once again
my life would flash before my eyes.........

          The Street Life explodes on the Night scene;
    and a young brother tries to catch that impossible dream
      Cadillac cars, Movie stars and Ho's with Lady-like looks,
       a Blind-man, a Liquor stand and a trick gets took...

Gangsters, players and real pimpish Pimps;
elaborate cocktails, manicured nails and girls with swaying hips
From the womb to the tomb is all you knew;
because the Street of broken Dreams is where you grew.

          And suddenly Boo-Yaaa! and a crack puff;
             and one more hit just isn't enough!
But you were all that plus a Bag of Chips; hip, slick and cool,
         and then that Dope Thing made its move...

Stuck like Chuck, down on your luck and not even a friend;
laying in a Dope house, a jailhouse at your wits end,
Shot-up, Smoked-up and sucking on some bad-ass wine,
came close to Death more than just a few times...

       A Hope to Die dopefiend, had become your story;
           with all the misery, pain, and worry,
     A Prisoner of your own mind... being so blind;
        until it was time... until it was time...!

Then, my poor mother was called down to the morgue to identify her son.

Well, I guess it just wasn't time for the miracle of change in my life that night. You would think that would be enough for any fool to realize there was something incredibly wrong, after I had been beaten, shot at, and declared dead from an overdose.

You have to understand the overwhelming power and insanity of the disease of addiction to know all these horrible, life threatening events that took place that night. I just couldn't stop the obsession to use. This vicious cycle, this insidious predator had taken over my mind, body and soul. The only thing on my mind, after my eyes opened and I realized I wasn't going to die, was where in the world I could find a bag of dope that time of night. Where could I find me another blast, another crack puff, another *damn drug*!

Chapter 2 **Dopefiend Players**

A few years had passed since the incident at Ed's Hotel. After leaving the County Morgue that frightful night, I got right back into traffic, right back into my addiction. I had this innermost belief at the time that, Pimps didn't Die, they multiplied. So instead of trying to seek help for my obvious drug problem, I went straight to the cooker. I was at the spoon by noon. I got to talking out the side of my neck, saying things like, "The Pimp God spared my life so I could pimp ho's because I was one of the chosen few. I had to do what I had to do. Because I was born to pimp hard... I was born to pimp ho's."

A summer breeze fell from a bottomless sky and a heat wave embraced Chino maximum security prison, in southern California. As I set there in Chino's west yard, playing dominoes with some of my partners, one of my homeboys said, "Nigga! Are you going to play, or do I have to get on the intercom and call one of the guards to make you play!" Laughter could be heard all over the prison yard, but rather than talk crazy to my homeboy, Pimping Lenny, I just played the last and winning bone and got up and said in a real, pimpish voice, "If you'd play these dominoes the way you say you pimp them ho's, you'd have the winning hand, Lenny." Then, laughter really boomed throughout Chino's west yard.

It seems that my parole officer and the Bakersfield Police Department had new plans for me. From 1981 to 1984, I had been in and out of the county jail. So, finally, the judge looked back into my adult record where in San Francisco I was charged with kidnapping, robbery and assault. Even though I was facing a misdemeanor and parole violation, the judge said to me, "I wish to God there was a law that would allow me to give you ten years today, Mr. Lindsay. But, I'm going to take the recommendation of the probation department and sentence you to the middle term, 16 months to three years in the state penitentiary, which means you will do two years minimum." The judge looked me right in my face, picked up my files in both hands, shook them at me and screamed, "I'm warning you, Mr. Lindsay, if you ever come before me again, it's going to be hell to pay. Now bailiff, get this man out of my sight."

As I walked the yard after the domino game had broken up, I thought about what the judge had said that day and a twisted frown fell on my lips as I spoke to Lenny, "Man, that judge wasn't playing with me, but homeboy, I got this game figured out this time."

For most of my life, every time I got into trouble or was put in jail, I hadn't a clue that it was my thinking that always caused my problems. It was always the police, the judge, my mother or my father. It was everybody's fault but my own. I just couldn't swallow the idea that I had a serious drug problem. So until I figured out that I was the problem in my life and that I was an addict, I would always end up my worse enemy and be a prisoner of my own mind, until it was time.

As I continued to walk the prison yard with Lenny, I said, "Pimping is all I know! What else can a pimp do but pimp ho's!? I've got to do like the pimp's before me. I've got to pimp by the book this time, homeboy! Yeah, Lenny, you know yourself that I constitute for a prostitute, and I'm real big on putting a wig on a pig, to get my money." My homeboy Lenny slapped my hand in agreement and spoke back to me, "Seville, man, that's why I gave you that name years ago, because you've got a style of pure elegance. Ever since I've known you, you've had class just like the Seville Cadillac."

Later, sitting in my cell, I was all caught up in my dreams to pimp ho's. It was almost time for me to be getting out. I was preparing not to make the same mistakes I made before. At the time, I thought all I had to do was back up on my drug use. Now, I thought I had the magic formula on the street game and it was clear where I had gone wrong before. I swore on everything that I loved not to let drugs or anything else bring me back to prison. *I'd hold court on the streets.*

While in Chino, I had a hustle with a store I ran. I had a few cronies that worked in the prison store, the canteen. Every week, when my lady came up to visit me, she'd sneak in bags of weed. Sometimes, it came by way of her mouth, sometimes it came wedged in her pussy. When the prison store was closed, I was still open. However, my store was quite expensive. For instance, if you bought a pack of cigarettes from me, it was two for one. With the drug sales, I was pulling in a prisoner's mint. In other words, I was hustling my ass off.

My lady was a bonafide mud-kicker whose name was Jewel. She came up every week, and every week, like clock work, she'd be knocking down the penitentiary gates trying to see me.

I met Jewel through a friend of mine in Los Angeles. She was an ex-ho, and the so-called pimp she had been with would beat on her every chance he got. She finally left him after many years of abuse and got with me. She told me that she liked my style and the romantic way I talked to her. She said that I was the first man that seemed to want her, just for her, and not her ability to make money.

Yes! Jewel was beautiful as well as talented in her art of making money. I remember when I first saw her, when she visited me in prison. Yeah, Jewel was beautiful, she was like a precious stone. I believe I fell in love with her hips. Damn! That girl had hips with the motion of an ocean. About five-foot-five, she stood in ho-boots, with black,

satin hair that fell to her shoulders. She was
twenty-nine, high-yellow with hazel brown eyes,
and fine as wine. Her lips were bitter sweet and a
fatal attraction to any man that watched her
exquisite smile. She had intoxicating, voluptuous
breasts that spoke of endless pleasure. Her shapely
body was like an hour glass that promised many
moments of sensuous delight. She was all of that
and much, much more.

While in prison, I saved every dime I had
because I knew all pimps had the finer things in
life. I thought that real pimps drove Cadillac cars,
wore diamonds and dressed in the very best of
clothes and I meant to be a real pimp in every
aspect of the word.

When the day finally came for my release from
prison, Jewel was at the gate waiting for me. I had
been down two calendars and I still remember that
moment as if it were yesterday. How fine my lady
looked as I stepped to the outside world. She had
an old Chevy, I think it was a '69 Impala. When
we reached the parking lot, I looked back at Chino,
and I could see the gun towers. The ancient, old,
gray buildings, the walls of despair, the barbed

wire fence, and the horrible pit of prison life. I said a silent prayer that day, never to come back to Chino. As she drove I spotted a liquor store on the side of the highway. Everybody knows when you first get out of jail, you owe it to yourself to get drunk, so we pulled up to the liquor store. My first drink has always been Cognac Remey Martin. You see, once again, I had to have what I thought was the very best and all pimps drink the very best of liquor.

My lady and I hit it off pretty good before we got to her apartment in Longbeach. She had a small one-bedroom apartment right off Longbeach Boulevard. When we arrived I knew I had to set the tone for lovemaking, I had to do like my teachers before me. I had to give her just enough lovemaking to get her sprung. I had to put all my years of experience on the line because I knew the first time we made love, I would either blow it or put locks on her ass. Or as pimps would say, I would either "Cop and blow" or "Cop, block and lock."

I noticed her apartment was small but very nice. There was a lavish, black, sable sofa with joining end tables, a dark, rich rug that covered every inch of her apartment, and a bathroom which had attire that matched with everything else. On the walls were African-Egyptian paintings of Kings and Queens, and black drapes hung in innocence to add to the lavish decor. I was genuinely impressed. As we walked into the bedroom there was a king size bed and on the bed were black covers and big, king-sized pillows. The usual dresser and drawer set was in place, with plants and other furnishings. What I noticed most of all was a small plate and mirror that set in the middle of the bed. There were several rocks of cocaine and a large free-base pipe in plastic baggies.

It was 1986, and up until now I really hadn't cared for crack cocaine that much. I thought since I shot dope most of the time, that somehow that made me better than crack-smokers. I thought a real dopefiend shot dope, so that put me in a different class and somehow I was supposed to be immune to this drug and its seemingly worse devastation.

At that time, free-basing was just getting a grip on the streets. Once again, I was the type of dopefiend you just couldn't miss. If it was powder, liquid, pill or rock and it got you loaded or drunk, eventually, I took it. Even though I said my drug of choice was heroin, when you got right down to it, it really didn't make any difference.

At the time, I knew little about the disease of alcoholism and addiction. I was an alcoholic and an addict, I drank to get drunk and I used drugs to get loaded, that was the bottom line.

After being in prison for two years and not being able to get laid, and now being here with this lady and all this dope brought a smile to my face. I thought, in my own twisted mind, that the Pimp God was truly blessing me. Jewel went into the bathroom and I could hear the shower running. Instantly my manhood aroused to the occasion but my addict behavior was more powerful than any female. I was like a country boy going to the city for the first time. I broke the cap on the Remey Martin and drank straight from the bottle. As the bitter liquid ran down my throat, I all but puked it up, but being afraid to lose my cool and my "look-good," somehow, I was able to keep the alcohol down. I stood there marveling at all the drugs that

set on the bed. In a few minutes, I could feel my
nerves settling and my confidence return. I said to
no one in particular, "What I need now is a good
shot of heroin. I wonder if Jewel knows any one
with a connection."

"Damn!" was all I could say as this beautiful
Black woman came out of the bathroom. All she
had on was a towel that fit her like a glove.
"Baby," she said, in an intoxicating voice, "do you
want to dry me off or do I have to do it myself."
In the same breath, she threw the towel at me. In
all honesty, I think my heart actually stopped a
beat. I still remember, no matter what I was
thinking, I just couldn't find any words to say. I
believe my mouth was moving but I couldn't hear
myself speak. Jewel was beauty in its essence, she
was exquisite, mesmerizing, a wonder in its true
form. She was everything any man could ever
want in a life time.

I wanted this lady real bad but I wanted a shot
of heroin even worse. So like a dopefiend, as I
dried Jewel's naked body off with trembling
fingers, I said; "Hey sugar, this is all cool and
everything but, I was wondering where I could cop

some heroin."

The thing I liked most about street women that have been in the life, was their ability to please their man. She didn't even look annoyed or upset, she just went over to the phone and dialed a number. The next thing I knew she was talking to the dopeman. About ten minutes later, I could hear a knock on the door. Jewel got in bed and asked me to answer the door. She told me that G-Money was at the door with a bag and that it had already been taken care of. I smiled inwardly, saying to her in a practiced tone, "Girl, you're definitely what the doctor ordered."

After I got the bag from G-Money, I went into the bathroom and fixed. As the drug worked through my body, I felt like I was in seventh heaven and God had risen me from the dead. When I stepped out of the bathroom, my lady had pulled the covers back and was lying very naked on the king-size bed. Her body was a mountain of sensuous curves. She was total ecstasy; behold, a Goddess of pleasure. Once again, my breath was taken away and I was in awe. We made love that night for hours and she showered me with gifts of sensuous delight. Her body fit mine like a groove in place. Our lovemaking was sheer magic in motion. We hit areas of love that can't be expressed with words. There was an invisible line we crossed that night that would take us to even greater depths of passion.

Two days later, we laid totally exhausted. We still had dope because I found out that the dope man was sweet on my lady and he kept us supplied with drugs at a very minimal price. I had drank, shot heroin and smoked crack for two days straight. Jewel wasn't real big on shooting drugs but she liked to freebase. She said it enhanced her sexual desires. As far as I was concerned, it was all big fun.

Looking at this fine, Black woman next to me still as lovely as ever, I said, "Hey girl! I've got to take care of some of my business, you know we can't stay in bed forever, you know what I mean?"

She purred back at me, "Seville, daddy! You take the car, I'm just going to lay here and rest because you really know how to put wear and tear on a girl. We girls aren't like men, I'll probably be sore for a week." She smiled at me with those

piercing, hazel eyes and went on to say, "You've
really got your groove on and that two year cherry
I busted was a little more than I expected. Damn,
Seville! I think you hit pay dirt. I'm not only
choosing again but I'm willing to pay choosing
fees. Yeah, baby, whatever I got is yours for the
asking."

Well, if I'll be Damned! The cat was out the
box, I had succeeded in putting locks in place. Like
my predecessors would say so eloquently, "Seville!
You have copped, blocked and locked, a job well
done." In the next month or so, pimping was big
fun because I had the gun. With the money I had
saved while in prison, the funds my poor old
mother had sent me, and the nest egg Jewel had
given me for choosing fees, I had enough to get a
proper wardrobe, a few diamonds, and a practically
new, money green Brougham Cadillac.

I'll never forget that day when I left Jewel in
bed. My second day out of prison, I was driving a
money green Brougham, wearing tailored suits I
had bought fresh off the rack and real diamonds I
got from a dope dealer I ran into. At this particular
time in my life, even though I was a dopefiend, it

appeared that I was using drugs successfully. I had the car, the clothes, and a bottom lady that was like Seattle Slew coming out of the gates to get my money.

I was thirty-six years old, had been married twice, and had a number of children. I was at the age where I thought I knew everything. I had all the answers and the answers I didn't have, I didn't let anybody know. Out of all the times I had been in and out of jail or the penitentiary, this was the first time it seemed that I was finally in control. I thought I was the shit.

It was late when I got back to my lady's apartment. When I drove up in front of the apartment complex I blew the deep Cadillac horn. When Jewel didn't run out like I thought she would, I pushed the expensive steering wheel up and eased myself out of the plush, mahogany seats. By this time, my girl was at the front, fully clothed with a look of anger on her face. I wondered in my twisted mind why this woman appeared to have an attitude. The first thing that came out of her mouth was, "Where in the fuck have you been!" And in the same breath, she said, "and where in the fuck is

my car at, nigga!" It really wasn't what Jewel said
that bothered me, but it was the tone she used.
Suddenly my brain locked with anger and when I
looked around there were other tenants checking us
out, trying to see what the commotion was all
about. All that did was add fuel to my anger
because one thing I couldn't stand was to be loud-
talked and disrespected by anyone.

Before Jewel knew anything, I was through the
door and on all fours on her ass. I laid hands on
her like I was fighting another man. I used brutal
force, first with my fists, then with my feet. I hit
her so hard that I could actually smell fear in the
air. Then, right in the middle of the floor, she
began to piss on herself. For some reason that
enhanced my anger. With pimping on my mind and
with a deadly intent, I started to stump a mud-hole
in this woman's ass. I thought all successful pimps,
at one time or another, had to do this. I thought I
had the secret ingredient prescribed in the Pimp
Bible.

My belief on pimping was you never let a ho
get out of line. With that in mind, I brutalized this
beautiful black woman. Before I realized it, she

was screaming, "Please! Please, Seville, daddy! Please... don't beat me like this... I didn't mean anything. I was just concerned, with you just getting out of jail, being on parole and being gone all day. I was worried that something had happened to you." When I looked down at the heap on the floor, she was in a fetal position. Like a child, Jewel was in a ball trying to ward off the blows.

Suddenly, a light went on, and I realized this beautiful lady of the night could be physically scarred from the terrible abuse I was causing. Like a slap in the face, fear set in. However, it wasn't normal fear like the fear of the police, parole officers or even the fear of going back to jail. No! It was different. It was the twisted fear realized by those pimps before me. "Ho's are merchandise for a price! Don't harm your merchandise!" In other words, if Jewel was harmed or scarred, that would affect money in my pocket.

So, like a true Boss Player, I recognized that I needed to use finesse in this delicate situation. I didn't want damaged goods on the street because this was the way I made my money. I reached down and lifted her gently in my arms. Face to face, I looked her dead in the eyes and said, "Girl, you know good and well I wasn't really trying to hurt you, I was just a little upset about the way you came at me. Baby, you know Seville ain't about to hurt his lady." So with that, I placed heated, passionate kisses on her neck, both of her cheeks and then her trembling lips. I took her to the bathroom and placed her under the shower, and then made love to her. We were caught up, again and again, in a blissful world of total passion.

One thing I learned about the street game was I thought I had to be this great actor, always showing control. I believed if I showed any weakness towards a woman it would cause harm to me and ruin my reputation as a real man.

Even though I was an addict and didn't understand the progression of the disease of addiction, I would learn my lessons about drugs being a symptom of my disease.

For a while, everything went pretty good. I had established quite a foothold on Jewel and had set her down on the ho stroll. However, the money was too slow for a woman ho'n. Also, I didn't want to admit it, but I was insanely jealous.

I remember one night, Jewel had been out on the track about an hour or so. I was hangin' out at one of the local night clubs when Jewel came running in, out of breath, telling me about this big score she had made. All that was real good, until she told me intimate details about what the trick had done to her sexually. That really bothered me, to know she had sex with somebody else. Unknowingly, I had made a grave mistake. I had allowed my feelings to get in the way. Somehow, I had actually fallen in love with this woman, but how can you love someone and treat them the way I treated her.

I had heard, from other pimps in the life, that a good thief was better than three ho's on their backs. So, the very next day, I had her drop her boosting hand. On a good day, Jewel was stealing two to three hundred dollars worth of merchandise. With my lady stealing to get my money, I didn't have to worry about what the tricks were doing to her.

I'll never forget the night when I was in an ugly mood. I had been reading one of Donald Goines' books, *Whoreson*. I had gotten to the part where the main character, Whoreson Jones, had gotten out of prison. He had run into a street ho named Ruby, that took him for a trick. He had put this brutal beating on her to show her the error of her ways. I had actually become the character Whoreson Jones, and I had planned in my twisted mind to take it to the next level.

Jewel had come in later than usual and she hadn't hit pay dirt. In other words, she hadn't made any money. So acting out the character, I made a pimp stick—two clothes hangers twisted together. While this beautiful, Queen of the Night was in the shower, I, like a crazy man in the throes of my addiction, started brutally beating her. I don't remember how long, but when I finished, I had become obsessed like the character Whoreson. I began to have brutal sex with her. It was like I was in someone else's body. I had become this other person. I had become an animal.

The next day, as I laid there next to my woman, I tried to make myself feel good about what had happened. To cover up my feelings about what I had done, I copped a fresh batch of heroin, and like an addict, I began to prepare my next fix. I very

delicately shook the brown powder from the small
baggy with the dexterity of an experienced
dopefiend. My fingers went to work striking
matches under the used bottle cap, where this
insidious drug lay in water. I found a vein right off
and watched the telltale blood rush into the syringe.
As I felt the heroin take affect, I began to feel
better about myself. A fog of euphoria took me to
heights where I didn't give a damn about anything
or anybody, including myself.

For most of my life, my feelings were very
difficult for me. Instead of facing any given
situation in my life, I would medicate my feelings
with drugs and alcohol. After that brutal assault on
Jewel that night, she had become very scared of
me. She never knew when I would strike out.
During this time in my life, I had become very
violent, and I really didn't understand why.

Jewel and I were together about six months.
The last time I saw her I was riding down on her.
She had just made a sting at a bank because she
was a professional when it came to cashing stolen
checks. She had gone in and cashed a five-
thousand dollar check she had beaten from some

old lady. When she hit the curb outside the bank, she started to run. Naturally, I thought something had gone wrong. Jewel was so frightened of me, when she saw me ride up on her, she kept running. When I finally caught up to her again, about five blocks from the bank, I slammed on my brakes, got out the car and put a gun to her head. I half dragged and half carried Jewel to the car. When I got her in the car, I threatened to kill her and break both her legs. I started driving home and I asked her what had happened. She started crying hysterically, and took the money from her purse and laid it on the seat next to me. She said she couldn't live like this anymore, and she wanted out. That night, while I laid in bed drunk and loaded, Jewel left me with just the clothes on her back. That was really just the beginning of the end.

Three weeks later, I found myself in the Los Angeles County Jail for possession of a controlled substance and a parole violation. To this day, I really don't remember what the hell happened. All I remember is that I had been up for six or seven days, shooting heroin and smoking crack twenty-four seven. The next thing I knew, I was in the penitentiary for another year of my life.

It seemed that I just couldn't understand that I had a drug and alcohol problem. I always thought that I could handle the drugs and the alcohol but it was like I heard somewhere in recovery, "One was too many and a thousand never enough." The life I was living could ultimately bring me to my death. If not death, then the jails, the institutions and the horrible pit of dereliction.

Here are some words that focus on what was really going on...

They say Dopefiend Players don't die,
they multiply,
but that's just a ghetto term, an old insidious lie;
so now you sit in a five by five,
and everyday and night you ask yourself
why?

But remember you were always so hip, slick and cool
drank your first bottle of wine, before you ever got in school.
Claimed to Pimp or Die, rest and dress;
drove Cadillac cars with the very best,

In your life time, you might've done a few of these things;
but as you look around now, you know they were only
impossible Dreams.
Dreams of your minds-eye, the old ghetto lie;
because Dopefiend Players do die, they don't multiply,

      they just Die.

           They just Die...

Chapter 3 **Black Woman**

From Mother Africa's Kings and Queens,
you came to me in a Black radiant dream;
a Goddess, an Angel, a thousand shooting stars,
sparkling through the Heavens, like the star that you are...

You were the Beginning and the End,
My Queen, my Princess, my Nubian friend;
you were the Birth of my Black People,
and even as a slave, you were made equal...

For 400 years, you cried out my name,
but I was so lost, so broken and so ashamed;
in a mire of fog with my back against the wall
you stood with me through the struggle, refusing to fall;

We were back to back, when Nat Turner was born,
and then came Harriet Tubman's Railroad, blowing it's Mighty
Horn!
It was Rosa Parks, that refused to get off the Bus,
to let America know, that in God We Trust!

Bessie Smith sang the Blues,
letting everybody know that we were here to stay, "Win or
Lose!"
Kathleen Cleaver spoke on the solution
while Angela Davis put the guns on the table, for the
Black Revolution...!

Black Woman; you were the Magic in Mahalia Jackson's voice,
letting the World know that God gave us a choice;
Nikki Giovanne's poetic expression,
put Black Folks on the move, in the right direction...

It was a Black Woman, that shared the Dream of King,
when he spoke the words of eloquence, "Let Freedom Ring!"
Coretta, Shirley Chisholm and let's not forget Maya,
that brought the Dream of King, just a little bit higher.

Sojouner Truth, put the Truth in velvety motion,
as far as the Seven Seas and beyond the Mighty Oceans;
So I ask you Black Woman: Mother Africa's Queens,
bring back the Kings, the radiant Dreams;
The shooting Stars with dreams of Kings & Queens

  Bring back the Dreams...
    Bring back the Dreams...
     Black Woman,
       Bring Back the Dreams...!

It was 1970, and falling rain seemed to be
swallowed by the immense prison yard at Duel
Vocational Institution. Some called it Tracy or
Gladiator School, whatever the name used for this
place, it was prison to me and many others. Tracy,
CA was a little, one-horse town, south of
Sacramento. The only thing I've ever known that
area for was the penitentiaries, namely San Quentin
and Folsom prisons.

It was the 4th of July, Independence Day, as I
laid there in my bunk, in J-Wing, asleep and
dreaming about all the proud Black Women in my
life. First, my mother Elizabeth Lindsay, who
nurtured me as a child, whom I loved more than
life itself. Then grandma Lindsay, my father's
mother, who I called Paw-Paw, a lady I cherished.
My grandmother Theresa Cooper, my mother's
mother, who said I would change and one day
preach for the Lord. All these women were very
important to me, at that time in my life. 1970 was
part of the Black Revolutionary era, and I had been
doing a lot of soul searching. I was twenty years-
old at the time, and as I dreamed, my dreams
started to focus on all the Black women heroes in

history. Angela Davis was speaking out at
Berkeley University, Kathleen Cleaver was
denouncing racism and Nikki Giovanni was
expressing velvety defiance towards social
oppression. These Black women had joined
together and were marching on Washington.

All of a sudden, I heard a loud clanging sound,
then voices saying "Lock down... lock down! All
inmates go to your cells immediately!"

"Damn!" was all I could say, as I woke up and
reality slapped me dead in the face. I was still in
Tracy doing time, and there were no women heroes
marching on Washington. I jumped off my bunk,
half asleep and scurried to the small window that
sat in the iron clad door. Looking through the
small window, I had to strain my eyes and press
my body in such a way, so that I could see what
was going on outside on the tier. I saw black
inmates running to make it to their assigned cells.
Some shit had hit the fan out in the yard.

Earlier that day, other black inmates and myself
had been celebrating Independence Day. Most of
the black inmates were out in the prison yard,
while this brother was reciting a powerful poem by

Claude McKay, entitled *Black Mother*. As he
recited the poem, the words were like incredible
waves of intensifying electrical sparks of fire,
igniting a powder keg of black people that seemed
to explode in mid-air. It seemed somehow unreal,
because all the brothers stood in unison, cheering
in an awesome awakening. Then, there was a
chilling, perilous, unholy wind that came from
nowhere and the yard became very still. Suddenly,
from the other side of the yard, I could hear racial
slurs, and words like, "SIEG HIEL! SIEG HIEL!
SIEG HIEL!" which the white Nazi's were saying
in a cowardly but dangerous manner. The Nazi
congregation wasn't moving, but they were
screaming obscenities and telling the blacks to go
back to Africa. The blacks began to rise and move
in perfect unison and became a powerful oasis of
Blackness. Then, from gun towers, you could hear
the guards over the intercom saying, "All Blacks
take it in, this is a lock down! All Blacks take it in,
this is a lock down!" At first some of the brothers
hesitated, then one of the brothers from the Black
Panther Party said, "It ain't over, but we can kill
whitey another day. Let's take it in stride, it don't

make sense to be shot down like animals today."
Then just like magic, all the black inmates began to
move in the other direction, towards their cells.

I'll never forget that day, because it could have
gone either way. There could have been a mass-
murder that day. Sometimes, I thank God for not
letting me be killed. There was something in the
air, I can't quite explain it in words, but it was
there—an ungodly, hostile and warlike presence
that had enveloped Tracy.

As this Black sea of inmates moved back to
their cells, there was talk of regrouping and when
lock down was over, we'd move on the Nazi
population and anybody else that stood in our way.
What happened was, that very day, the brothers got
restless and made their move on anything white,
including the guards.

I said a silent prayer as I looked through my
cell window. I could see black inmates literally
being cut down by the goon-squads. It was my
understanding that we weren't supposed to make a
move until lock down was over.

As bad as I wanted to be a part of the uprising,
the other black voices had voted on me not to

participate. They thought since I was a short timer, doing only a couple of years, and being a strong voice against the social ills of Black racism, it was best that I took the Black struggle and the message to the streets. At that time in my life, I was considered a Black Revolutionary, a Black Militant. I was thought of as a leader and one of the voices at Tracy because for most of my life, I'd always had a strong influence on people. I was good at speaking out about how I felt. I knew that racism existed in our country, and I was speaking-out every time and everywhere I got the opportunity.

In the weeks that followed the uprising, three blacks and one white were killed. Tracy was locked down and there were reports on the television, radio and the newspapers. But the media has always put out to the public the authorities version of the situation. That version was everything but the truth, and that's *the truth*.

While I was in Tracy, I read and studied like my life depended on it. I was so brain washed by the system and my addiction. My world was very limited and the only thing I was sure of was that I

was black, locked-up, and somewhat hopeless. I
was a black man in a world I really knew little or
nothing about. While I was incarcerated, the most
educational and profound book I read was the
Autobiography of Malcolm X. It gave me a very
different perspective on life. My hero's became
Malcolm X, Eldridge Cleaver, Martin Luther King,
Jr., Angela Davis, Kathleen Cleaver and many
more.

There was a part of Malcolm X's autobiography
where he talked about his drug addiction and
alcoholism. I started to see my similarities with his
story and figured I might be able to change as well.
So like Malcolm X, I went through the dictionary,
taking it apart and learning everything I could
about the English language. I also began to study
many philosophers such as Mao, Marx and Lenin.
My mind began to really open up and I started to
understand why capitalism in the western world
wasn't working. On Saturday mornings, I'd
faithfully talk about what I had studied in a black
studies group. I was fascinated with political
science and the many answers it exposed. I found
out that the penitentiary could be an asset, instead

of a liability, in my life. I studied so much that I would get migraine headaches. Exhausted from studying day and night, I'd be literally blown away. Sometimes I'd have to make myself go to sleep before I passed out. I was so engrossed in my studies, it seemed that I was hypnotized at times. This institution, this penitentiary, had become a university to me in some respect.

In the morning hours, I'd position myself facing the East and pray to Allah. So, like Malcolm X, I had taken the same step by becoming a Muslim. It's really amazing how disciplined this faith had made me. I, for the first time, had discovered that I no longer had a desire to use drugs. I had become committed to this belief and I had become an example of a Black militant Muslim. It seemed that I had finally found the solution.

It's really funny now, as I reflect back on my past. I would always get myself together while I was locked-up. But the minute I hit the street, every single time, no matter how good my intentions were, I would always end up using drugs. I'd be right back in that horrible pit of addiction, all over again.

I remember the summer of 1969, when my
parents thought it would be beneficial for me to go
to San Francisco and live with my aunt. She was
also an alcoholic, but she kept a job and was
responsible. It appeared she had her life together.
On the very day I got to San Francisco, after
promising my parents I would never drink again, I
was drinking again. As a matter of fact, when the
Greyhound Bus made it's first stop, I went straight
to the liquor store and got me a bottle of vodka. I
thought vodka was breathless, but little did I know,
any kind of alcohol would smell, especially if you
drank it like I did.

My arrival in San Francisco was awesome. I
was nineteen-years-old, and I remember the bright
city lights were electrifying. I meant to take the
world by it's tail and throw it in any direction I felt
best. I felt I was in control again and I meant to
really get into the fast life.

When I finally made it to my aunt's house, I
had been drinking, but I still had somewhat been
able to manage my actions. My aunt was a very
sweet lady, but she was a hipster. She'd party at
night and get up and go to work faithfully the next

morning. Sometimes, though, she'd over do it and all hell would break loose. She was a registered nurse with all the qualifications and she was able to hold a job. She had a nice house, car, expensive clothes and most of all, she had her groove on.

I had been at my aunt's house about three weeks, and had a job in the making at the ship yard. One night, I was on the corner of Filmore and Haight, right in front of the well known night club, The Giant Glass, which was where a lot of pimps and players spent time. I was out of money, down on my luck and full of Golden Gate white port wine. I had also been taking the infamous drug known as red devils, gorilla cookies, or fender benders. It had many names, but it's effects were devastating on whoever took them. Cocaine and heroin had also become my daily maintenance drugs.

Now remember, I was supposed to be adopting the career of pimping, but that was short-lived because of my addiction. There I stood, in the explosively lit-up city of San Francisco. I was loaded to the point of no return with the mentality of a hope-to-die dopefiend. I was ready to get mine, by any means possible, by any means necessary. I was desperately willing to take my situation to the next level. I was on a suicidal mission.

I'll never forget that night in August of 1969. There was a passing car with a white dude in it. Suddenly, I walked up to the car and snatched the door open. Getting in the car, I put the empty wine bottle under my coat and played it off, like I had a gun. I told the driver in the meanest voice I could, that this was a robbery, so don't make it a murder. I had no fear. Even though I didn't have a gun, I would have bottle beat the driver to death. It was really amazing, because the driver had just gotten out of the penitentiary himself. He emptied his pockets to let me know he had no money. Not wanting to be out done, I got this brilliant idea. Why not him and I team up and rob somebody else? Damn! That had to be the craziest idea I could possibly think of.

So, as we rode towards the Tender Loins district, for some reason I thought this was sound judgment. Not to mention, this white dude was over six-feet tall and weighed about three-hundred pounds. I had to be totally insane. I must have been seeking a Death Wish in every area of my life.

When we reached the Tender Loins district, I spotted this old man walking down the street. He looked like a good mark, so in my most hip, slick and cool expression, I told the driver to pull over. Sliding out the car, like a true gangster in motion, I came up beside the old man and said, "Give me your money or your life, it doesn't matter what comes first." That old man was definitely no punk, because after he made no indication of going for his wallet, I hit him with a superfly hook and a mack'n gangster, right cross.

You see, I was always cool in whatever I did. Being cool was part of my basic make-up, everything I did had to be cool. I was a living testament of coolness and anything else was alien to me.

I was a little too cool, though, because after I hit the old man and was reaching for his wallet, I didn't see the Sunday Punch he came at me with. The white dude in the car had long gone up the street. Then, San Francisco's finest hit a corner

and came down on me in the commission of a
crime.

    To illustrate that particular time in my life, I
wrote this poem entitled, *Live and in Living
Color...*

The Dice rolls seven...hit eleven!
and a spike in your arm and you think you're in heaven;
it's a vicious-cycle, right before your eyes
as you fall in the Net of the Spider and the Fly...!

Driven by a force more powerful than man;
this cancerous-puss...the drug of the Damned!
Heroin, horse, speed or cocaine,
it's all about pain, whatever the name...

Your drug of choice was always more!
from a bottle of wine, to the Corner Liquor Store
a Legend in your own mind,
that's why you thought you had to have it, One More Time.
But the Clock runs out you'd soon discover,
that Drugs ain't no play thang, they're Live and in Living Color.

In your life time you'd beat a man, woman or Beast!
you'd even steal from your poor old father, if he wasn't
deceased.
Mama, Daddy, brother or wife
you had become an animal, in this thang called Life...!

I had become an animal and the San Francisco Police Department had plans on caging this animal up. The old man that I tried to rob that night suffered minor injuries and would testify against me a month later. It had to be God working in my life again, because while I sat there in San Francisco County Jail for robbery, assault with intent to cause great bodily harm, and kidnapping, the police had knocked down my aunt's door. They had a warrant for my arrest for the murder of a police officer. It seems that one of my so-called friends had killed a policeman while robbing a liquor store. He had conveniently placed my identification, which I had lost, at the scene of the murder. I remember my mother struggling with telling me the details of how the police drew their guns while looking for me.

As we talked in the visiting room, she was crying. She had been trying to get me out on bail, and we both realized that even though it looked bad for me, God was working a miracle in my life. That miracle happened, and I would go to court on reduced charges and end up with two years in Tracy.

My mother and grandmother were always there for me. I remember one time, while I was in Tracy, my mother caught a bus with my cousin Desiree. It was raining cats and dogs, but mostly dogs, that day. They had gotten off at the wrong stop or the bus had broke down or something, and it had been about a ten mile walk to the institution. When she walked into Tracy, it was another institution, another visiting room. I could hardly believe my eyes, my mother was soaking wet and crying uncontrollably. She told me what happened as she clutched my hands to hers and she asked me to promise her that I would never go back to jail again. I made a solemn pact with her that day. I really meant to never return to prison again.

After my release from Tracy in February of 1971, I would again go back into the nightmares of addiction, and be right back where I said I'd never go again. During my two years in Tracy, the world kept changing but I didn't. As soon as I got out, I'd be throwing rocks at the penitentiary gates trying my best to get back in.

When I made that solemn pact with my mother that day. I went back to my cell and wrote these

words as a testimony of my faith, and to reaffirm
my love to her and all Black Women. Here are the
Notes To My Black Mother:

Out of the cold blackness;
a shadow with eyes casting fire and flame,
has taken the blame, you dwell in shame;
so refined... so untamed...

Your silken black skin pressed against the chains;
no one can hear your staggering tears,
so alone, caressed by years...

Forgive me, Black Mother!
for I have been asleep for 400 years,
and as I wipe the matter from my eyes;
I begin to cry, and sigh, I lay there and Die...

As I lurk from the Lion's Den;
I see you Black Mother once again,
as a fist, as an arm;
a raging Militant Storm...

I see Black against White;
violence in the night,
a New Day in sight...

I see the Liberating truth;
of Sojourner Truth,
the fiery Railroad of Harriet Tubman;
and the zeal,
that all Black Women feel;
when they mount the Liberating Wheels
of *Angela Davis* and Bobby Seal...

Who surge on;
through grief and scorn,
so that one day, we will see
the Day to be Free!

There is a howling in the night;
Niggas are in fright,
Black Mothers help us fight!
The Heavens fall from the sky;
    Niggas die, while other Niggas cry,
       but Niggas are me;
          and *Black Mother*, we must be Free...!!!

I dedicated those words to my mother,
Elizabeth Lindsay, almost thirty years ago, in 1971.
But little did I know that God was preparing me,
even then, for a much greater message.

Chapter 4 **25 Years to Life**

It was 1992, and there I sat in another dope-house in Bakersfield, California. I had just gotten out of the Kern County Jail. I had only been out a month or so, and one more time, I was trying to figure out where I could hit me a lick to get this dope sickness up off my ass.

It was Sunday morning, and as I looked around the small room, I saw empty Night Train bottles, a couple of crack pipes converted from car antennas, wine bottle caps used for cookers, and a bloody, stopped up syringe with no dope in sight. Debris scattered the nasty floor, and right in the middle of an old soiled mattress lay a bare-assed hooker named Tenders that I copped the night before on a dope-run. Suddenly, my minds-eye began to play tricks on me and a frown came to my lips. I had a moment of clarity and saw where drugs had always took me.

Everyday since I had gotten out of jail, I had been on a death mission. At first, it was fun drinking and getting loaded. But here I was once again, forty-two years old and I had nothing to show for my life. My kin folks wanted nothing to do with me, because every chance I got I'd either be begging them for money or trying to figure out how I could steal from them. I was always loaded or drunk or a combination of both. I had made a fuck'n mess of my life and drugs and alcohol had always brought me to my knees.

My primary drug at the time was heroin. That gorilla was doing flips on my back and I knew I had to make a move real quick. That gorilla quickly grew into a full grown beast. He wasn't bullshittin', he meant to be fed. This beast didn't give a damn about what I was feeling, or who I beat, cheated or stole from. I believe at that very moment I would have sold my soul to the devil for a hit of dope.

I heard in recovery, that drug addiction was cunning, baffling and powerful. It's not the amount of drugs one takes that matters, it's the reaction in the body and the obsession in the mind. Any mind altering substance taken by an addict or alcoholic sets him off on a spree, and no amount of self-will or human aid can stop this. It's been my experience that the only way to stop such a spree, has to come from a higher power, a power greater than oneself. For me, that power came from what I choose to call God.

That morning, at that moment, I didn't care for the prospect of God doing anything for me. I was in a space where I had to get fixed by any means necessary. I didn't care what I had to do, but I knew I had to do something. Shortly after considering my options, I thought about ol' faithful, my mother. Yeah, she was always good for a few dollars. Besides, I had some money coming in the mail from an old lawsuit. I had been hurt years ago in an industrial accident and a big check was on its way, the lawyer said it would be a few days. So with desperation in my heart, I called my grandmother's. My mother had just left for church. I was in such a hurry and so confused that I didn't realize my grandmother told me that my mother had left some money for me. My check had come, but she couldn't get it to me until tomorrow.

To this day I don't know how I missed that part of the conversation. I must have really been in bad shape.

    After I hung the phone up, I decided to drop my boosting hand at the neighborhood corner 7-11. When I got to the store I went straight to the wine section. I figured a bottle of wine would always go good whatever else happened that day. So, I stuck a bottle of Night Train Express in my pants, and before I made it to the door, I decided I needed some cigarettes as well. So I went up to the counter where cartons of cigarettes were on display. I boldly reached for a couple of cartons, not really caring who saw me. I put the merchandise under my coat and went through the door. All hell broke loose! As I was going through the door, the manager who had been watching me the whole time from behind one of the coolers screamed at me, "Stop! Stop! You hear me, I said stop! I'm going to call the police!" He must have really been nervous about his job because he was actually running after me. When I was boosting at that time, I always kept me a can of pepper spray. It was always better than carrying a gun or going into a boxing match with someone. So, I turned around, pulling out my pepper spray, and sprayed his ass real good. He stopped dead in his tracks and seemed to turn colors. He continued to scream and holler in my wake, "Stop! You hear me you son-of-a-bitch! You son-of-a-bitch, you!" I started laughing my ass off, more from fear than anything else. I just continued to laugh like nothing mattered. That fool ass manager was holding his face with both hands. By this time, his face had turned bright red, and him being a white dude, really made all the difference in the world. What the white dude should have done was just got on the phone and called the police. I ran across California Avenue laughing my ass off. I headed back to the dope-house down the street, where I had been laying my head for the last few days.

The apartment building was on the west side of town, the Palm Apartments or something like that. California Avenue was generally middle-class until you got to the east side which was predominately black. I was staying about a mile off of Union where most of the ho's worked.

When I got back to the apartments, I stopped to catch my breath in the parking lot. I was trying to calm my nerves from all the excitement, so I got behind a trash bin and took me a drink, if that's what you want to call it, because I had a long throat and I drank it about half way before I brought the bottle down. Damn! It tasted awful as I placed the top on the bottle. Once the alcohol began to take affect, I began to feel a little better about my troubles.

I had to climb some stairs to reach apartment 209, where I was staying. Before I got to the door, a head showed through the curtain and the door opened.

Mostly all dope-houses have a certain code they go by. There's usually someone watching the door and another person watching from the window. That way, there's a certain amount of protection put on the house and those in it.

When I entered the apartment, one of my dealer partners was there. He gave me a dime bag of heroin and a taste of cocaine. He told me not to worry about the money, he knew I was good for it. But like all dope dealers, he gave the impression that he needed his money as soon as possible.

Damn! That beast was doing triple flips by this time. So, with no hesitation, I went into the bathroom and began to fix. As I fixed the heroin and cocaine, I played with the spike, drawing the blood back and forth so as to make sure I didn't overdose. I jacked-off the syringe, not shooting all the drugs in my arm at once, allowing myself to see how potent the drugs were because I was a true fiend in every aspect of the word.

My eyes closed and the unholy world of a dopefiend brought me temporary freedom. I sat there in total euphoria, no more worries, no pain... no gain. The insidious life I lived as an addict, the jail houses, the penitentiaries, the near deaths, all of these things had been mysteriously removed from my mind. At that very moment in time, I was free.

From a distance, I heard someone saying, "He's in there!" I could hear screeching car wheels as the euphoria disappeared. All of a sudden, the thin, wooden door of the restroom came crashing in. All I could say was "Damn, here I go again!" as uniformed police came through the door. There were so many police I thought they were shooting Police Story and I was the infamous Al Capone.

The neighbors in the apartment complex had

been watching apartment 209. When they saw me
going up the stairs suspiciously that day, they
hurried and called in on me.

After my arrest, the ride wasn't long to the
Lerdo Facility, a.k.a. Kern County Jail. I had been
to jail many times, but now, there was a new law,
the three-strikes law, which was meant to crack-
down on the habitual criminal. Many of my
friends were made examples by this law.

As soon as I entered the Lerdo Facility, there
was this big, muscle-bound lady that looked so
much like a man, I started to call her sir. Her
words almost scared me to death. In a nasty voice,
she hollered that I was a very good candidate for
the three-strikes law. She said, "You there! You're
going down for a long time, MISTER! You're one
of the first candidates for the three-strikes law and
I hope like hell, you don't enjoy your stay, you
bastard you!" She gave me an ugly sneer and led
me to lock-up.

That night was very critical in my life. I
thought, on everything I loved, that finally the
judicial system was going to wash me away, like
"Josh-a-way." I remember calling my grandmother

and mother on the phone. I talked to my grandmother first, telling her my situation. She said in a voice almost unknown to me, "Savon! I'm so, so, so sorry, boy! There was money over here for you. Your mama left some money over here for you. I'm so sorry for you."

It was Sunday night, and my mother had been at church all day, and as I talked to my grandmother, my mother came in the house. I was talking to the two women that cared most about me in my life.

I felt I was in my *Last Days*. We called the courts on the three-way, and the lady on the other line said I was on the morning docket for felony court, Division F. She also said, with all the focus on this new law, that they had three-strikes attached to my file. I couldn't believe what was happening to me. Some of the other inmates were preparing their cases, and some had already struck out. Some were advising me how to fight my case. They were jail house lawyers, fighting for their lives. There I was, scared to death, not knowing a damn thing to do.

I got on the phone again about 11:00 p.m., the

eleventh hour. My grandmother and mother told me that it was going to be all right. They said that both of them had prayed some special prayers for me and God was going to take care of everything. They told me not to worry, that God was taking care of business.

Now, of course I didn't want to believe none of that God stuff. I was trying to convince these two ladies that I needed some bail money or if nothing else, a damn good lawyer. The last words I heard on the phone that night were, "God is all you need. So get somewhere and get still, get on your knees and pray."Later on that next morning, about three a.m., I got on my knees and prayed. I didn't really believe that prayer was going to work for me, but I prayed anyway. I don't remember exactly what I said, but I remember I was very sincere. I got in my bunk and took my ass to sleep. Considering everything, I slept better than I had in days.

It was about five in the morning when the jailer started calling names for the court calendar. Even though I had been through this jail routine many, many times, and had been doing time for many, many years, that particular morning was exceptionally emotional for me. Being chained to the rest of the inmates and walking down that corridor was an experience I can't explain in words. As I walked with the rest of the inmates, I thought about how drugs and alcohol had destroyed my life. I began to pray again that morning and I asked God to simply "Help me!"

That was the beginning of my surrender to a God as I understood him.

I continued to walk until I heard the jailer call my name. "Savon...Charles...Lindsay! You, come with me to misdemeanor court." He took the handcuffs off me and directed me to another court room. My first thoughts were that they had made a mistake or something as I stood there in Division G, misdemeanor court of the Kern County court house. The judge read off the charges. He didn't mention any felonies of any kind. No pending charges, none of that. He just asked me how did I plea to a misdemeanor, petty theft charge?

Right at that moment, my addict mind went to work. My son had gotten shot down a few days before I went to jail. So now, even though I loved my son and felt bad about his death, I thought that, just maybe, this judge might give me a break. So I asked him with sheer desperation, "Your Honor! My son was shot down in the street the other day, and I'd like to see him and help with his burial. I'd like to ask your Honor, if it's humanly possible, to be lenient enough to give me some time on the street with my family in these painful times?"

Suddenly, the judge started laughing as if I had said something amusing. "Mister Lindsay! I'll say one thing for you, you've got Balls! You know, Mister Lindsay, you've been in my court room so many times, I almost feel like we're kin folks or something." I didn't recognize this judge at the time but undoubtedly, he knew me. He went on to say, "Here you come, just escaping the habitual criminal act, your felony charges were dropped to misdemeanors, and now you ask me for a break, some leniency?" He smiled down at me and shook his head saying something incredibly unbelievable. "Do you come from a praying family?" I looked up at him with a sincere face and said, "Yes, your Honor! And I'm a praying man myself." "Well," he said, "this is what I'm going to do, and I don't really understand why I'm doing it. But I'm going

to exonerate you from all charges. I want it to be
stipulated that if you ever come in this court room
again and I'm sitting on this bench, I'll give you
the stiffest term I can. You'll regret the day you
ever seen me, and prayer won't mean a thing." At
that point, I bowed my head and silently thanked
God. From that experience, I wrote these words...

Tears... Cries and Fears...!
the sound of Sir*eee*ns, a child's troubled dreams;
street corners are full of young desperate boys,
drugs and guns their only toys...

The Ghetto Term, the spoon by noon;
but to be fixed by six could be your doom,
so many minds deranged;
the Mighty White Rock, the deadly cocaine...

Young innocent girls displaying their bodies and wares;
but in the "Dope Game" no one really cares,
city streets congested with so much confusion;
Dead-end streets with dreams of delusion...

Middle class whites and Blacks as well;
fall every time, under this Deadly spell,
it's a drug so sinister, so ugly in speech;
Europe... Asia... the entire World, it's mighty reach...

This drug has been known to take many things;
and if you don't watch yourself, it'll even take your Dreams,
it will take your pride possessions, fine clothes, and pretty cars;
it's been known to take many a man down, even Movie Stars,
just like Richard Pryor's fire that time;
igniting his body and almost his mind...
They say "King Heroin," had that insidious bite;
but that *Glass Pipe*, is more hideous, just by sight,
like a deadly cobra, slithering in your path;
One Crack Puff could be your last...

Flake... Rock... Crank!
a hideous monster, a ghastly mistake,
this drug will make you steal from your own mother!
your family and friends and many others...

It will make you forsake a newborn baby!
lash out at others and get you maybe?
So just be aware of this *poisonous "White Hope...!"*
it will take your *morals* and your whole world, "Blown up in
Smoke...!"
and the moral of this story is like a horrible maze,
that's why it's called, *The Last Days... The Last Days...*
The Last Days...!

Once again, God had done for me what I could not do for myself. I knew in my innermost soul at that time, that I should have spent the rest of my life in some rat hole institution in California.

Chapter 5 **Welcome to Fresno**

T hat night, after the judge had cut me loose from all the charges, I decided to catch the first thing smoking, to put some distance between me and that judge. I thought, if I ever faced that judge again, the next time I wouldn't be so lucky. I'd end up with "The Big Bitch," which was the inmates slang for 25 years to life.

After my mother and a friend of hers picked me up at the Kern County jail, I told my mother to take me straight to the Greyhound Bus station. Since the judge had cut me loose, it didn't make any sense for me to hang around Bakersfield and take any more chances. My addiction was doing one handed push-ups as we rode from the jailhouse to the Greyhound Bus station. I asked my mother several times to stop so I could get me a drink.

It was about one in the morning before I got out of jail, but the only thing on my mind was getting a drink or a drug. It didn't matter that I had just escaped another life threatening situation. It didn't matter that my son had been killed recently. It didn't matter that the judge had let me go to bury my son. It just didn't matter! What mattered was feeding my addiction.

For years, the only thing that mattered to me was getting fuck'n loaded. My mother could have fallen dead, my father could have been dying on his sick bed, my children could have died in some horrible accident. All of these traumatic things could have taken place in my life, but my addiction and alcoholism were so powerful that it told me that none of these things mattered. Nothing mattered but to feed that insidious beast.

My disease had a contract out on my ass and it would slowly bring me to my knees.

My mother finally got me on the bus without a drink or a drug. But, by the time I got to Fresno, it was way past time for me to get loaded. At that time, Fresno was the dope capital of the United States, per capita. The thing I knew for sure, was that it had the cheapest prices on drugs I've ever known. If you had three to six dollars, you could buy a nice size bag of heroin or cocaine. It really didn't matter how much or how little money you had, you could find it in "The 'No"—Fresno.

I had an older cousin that lived in Fresno
named Al, at least that's what I called him. He was
as tough as they come where the street life was
concerned. He was a true legend in our family on
my father's side because of his uncanny skills as a
hustler. He could get a dollar out of a mule's ass
sitting down or water from a dry well. He was like
a black Al Capone in my life at that time. I really
admired Al, he was one of my role models and I
wanted to be just like him.

In Fresno, the west side was where I'd always
end up. Most of the heroin was on that side of
town and my cousin Al lived there. My first stop
was the liquor store. I remember getting a bottle of
Night Train Express, because this was the wine my
cousin drank. At first, I had a little trouble finding
my cousin's house. It had been a while since I had
been there, and my cousin was always on the
move. I ran into a local dealer and as I copped
from him, I asked him about my cousin. He told
me that Al was running a Ho house right off Fresno
Street. Damn! Al was always on top of his game
and staying in the mix.

As a walked up on Al's house, I saw him in the

front yard. When he looked up, he smiled and ran up to me and gave me a bear hug. He was about five-foot-nine, weighing a little over two-hundred pounds. He had a large nose from our Indian ancestry, brown eyes that spoke of joy but yet pain, and lips that gave you the impression that he could talk shit. Even though he was bigger than me, you could definitely tell that we were kin to each other. Some people called us the gangster twins because we looked so much alike and because we were both dopefiends. We also shared the same dreams in terms of the *street life*. Our life styles were so similar, but the bottom line was, we were both addicts.

The party was on as soon as I stepped through the door. We partied twenty-four/seven, all day and all night. I had a few hundred dollars that my mother had given me, and with the money from the insurance company, it appeared that I wouldn't be having any money problems for a while. I shot, smoked and drank for days on end until passing out. Then I got up and started the process all over again.

Finally, my money got short and real funny in a

few weeks. I started going on the street and
looking for anybody I could beat or rob. I started
boosting and stealing out of stores. It got real ugly
for me, but I was determined to turn the game
around. I ran into a lady that called herself Green-
eyes. We hooked up like real gangsters trying to
play the streets. Green-eyes was a bad ho, booster
and a true artist of the street game. My cousin Al
had rented me out the basement of his house. For a
while, that worked out real good, but my addiction
got so bad that I started stealing from him and
anybody else that got in my way.

You see, I was a hope-to-die dopefiend. I
didn't have a clue about handling my addiction. I
continued to go down this hopeless path of
destruction. God only knew how far I'd go until
I'd be willing to do what it took to turn my life
around. It seemed, the only direction for me was
the jails, institutions, dereliction and death. Or, I
could reach out for help and surrender to God and
get into recovery.

One night, me and Green-eyes went out and
made a pretty big sting. We had knocked this old
man in the head and took his money. We scored

about three grand and bought a lot of dope. We sat around nodding, scratching, shooting, smoking crack and drinking brandy. We were also trying to figure out how we could sell drugs without becoming our best customer.

Four days later, we were laid up in bed, broke, disgusted and dope-sick. Green-eyes went out trying to hit a lick and got busted. I decided to clean up my act and started going to 12-step meetings. Then, the first of the month came, and my mother sent to me a check I had been getting for compensation from a job I had been hurt on. As soon as the check came, my clean-up act went straight out the window. Once again, I could see where my life was going.

One night, I was sitting in the basement of my cousin Al's house. I was tired of being sick and tired of where my life was going. I looked in the mirror and saw this person I didn't recognize. It was me! I weighed about ninety pounds, soaking wet. My face was sunk-in and my eyes and head looked too large for my body. I was in shambles and had been swallowed up by my uncompromising disease of addiction. I looked

like a scarecrow or a broom stick with two big
eyes. I was fucked up. I wallowed in my own
sickness that night; hopeless, helpless and lost. I
thought about an old friend of mine named Reggie,
that died a dopefiend's death, and for some reason
this picture flashed before my eyes........................

A Cry of pain rushes out of you;
but few understand the things you do,
a Bottle of wine a bag of dope;
it's all the same insidious hope...

The sickness of wine swallowed like a treasure;
and the feeling it entails is so impossible to measure,
Late Night, neon signs and sho'nuff to the curb;
your body trembles for Iris Rose, Tokay or the Mighty
Thunderbird!

Today is like the first Day of your life;
as you cuddle the *Spike* just like you would your wife,
there's no turning back and nothing seems to be in sight;
just another Dopefiend, just another night...

Sheer madness rushes across your mind;
institutions, jails or Death you're so sure to find
young crazed kids selling rocks right up the street;
and one more hit on the Pipe and you're dead on your feet...

It's impossible to really define in words;
but this Dope thing isn't just a fantasy or something I heard
it's a slow murderous death that hits you like a charm;
a Pipe in your mouth or a Spike in your arm...

Young babies lay hungry and alone in bed;
no food on the table, not even a piece of bread,
the pipe... the spike... a wine bottle intact!
one more Day of madness for an addict...

The 'Ho Stro' and young pretty tenders on the go;
the Street Life, mini skirts and pretty fine bodies to show,
but there's a turning point and no real hope;
back on the track and another bag of dope...

A death wish turns the tide around;
and the promise of death has you wired for sound,
what's really going on, and you didn't even think,
and now you're searching for your last Dying drink.

A graveyard is now your resting place;
a few tears here and there and dirt thrown in your face,
but you "Reap what you Sew" and you made your life real
mean;
    and now you've seen the
        Death
           of
                a
                    Dopefiend...

My friend Reggie died the death of a dopefiend in the early nineties, and I would have died the same death if I had continued living like I was living. But today, years later, he lives spiritually in my heart. In my words there is a message of hope that no addict has to die from the horrible disease of addiction...

PART 2

Chapter 6 **A Lady Called Mama**

A Lady in all the wonders of her ways;
giving me a Special Love, as far back as my child days,
Mama, you were always there for me;
especially when I needed you most,
from the time I opened my eyes, your love for me,
you'd boast...

A Lady, a woman, a Mother to her son;
you were always there, you were that so Special one,
sometimes you'd tell me such Beautiful Stories;
about your love, your pain, your often time worries...

The Lady of my Life, *my Black Mother of Queen's*;
Mama, you'll always be there, even in my far existing dreams,
When I fell short on things, you told me to stand tuff;
be a Man, do the best you can;
Mama, you told me some Mighty Good Stuff...

There were times in coming up where I needed a good *word*;
and today, I'm a man because of what you told me, the things I
heard,
your wisdom and strength, sometimes hard to trace;
but when I do life today, I do it for you and Gods
blessed grace...

When I was on my sick bed, not having a *prayer*;
not my brother or my sisters but my Mama was always there,
Mama, you're just the Star that you are;
and just being your son has made me go far,
so I tell you Today with no hidden drama;
I Love You Girl, because you're My Mama...

I remember as a child, I'd wake up in the mornings and find my mother on her knees praying. My mother was always praying, because she'd tell me it was better to be prayed up than prayed out. She was a strong, black woman with more faith than I thought possible.

She'd take me to church with her every chance she got ever since birth. She'd say she saw something worth saving in me. She believed that God had a special task for me. She and my grandmother—her mother—always said that one day I'd preach for the Lord and help people. My mother was the true artist of the family. I believe she could have been another Mahalia Jackson. She was always writing; either a song, a poem, or a play, or singing at one of the church functions. One time, this big record company was interested in my mother's work. She could have been making records and singing all over the country, but my mother said her work was in her church fellowship. She was also very loyal to her family—her two sons, her husband, mother, father, sister and brothers—because she felt her family needed her most.

My mother was my first hero, because every time I'd see her, I'd see her strength and courage. She was always a beacon of hope and she walked her talk. Whatever came out of her mouth, she would show through her actions.

I was very sickly as a child because I had tuberculosis that I had contracted from my Uncle Pat. My mother used to take me to the hospital two to three times a week. One of the doctors that had been treating me, told her if I didn't get any better they were going to have to send me to a hospital way up in the hills somewhere, an institution that specifically dealt with people who had tuberculosis. At that time in the 1950s, there wasn't a whole lot of knowledge concerning that illness. If it seemed you weren't improving, they just sent you off somewhere until they figured out what to do with you. My mother wasn't too understanding of that idea. She believed that God could do anything, so she, my grandmother, and the church started praying. I'll never forget what she told me the next time she took me to see the doctor. She said the doctor told her a miracle had taken place because there was almost no trace of

the tuberculosis. Once again, God was working
miracles in my life. I often wonder why my
mother, and especially my grandmother, believed
in me when I didn't believe in myself, and why
God spared me so many times while I was in my
addiction.

Since I was so sickly as a child, I had a home
teacher that would come out and give me
schooling. When I was finally healthy enough for
public schooling, my mother brought me to my
first class. She'd tell me, "Now, boy! Don't you
get up here acting a fool, because I got something
for your foolishness out on the back tree at the
house." But as soon as my mother would leave the
school, I'd start acting out. It seems I was always
getting into trouble; stealing, fighting or something.
I remember when I was about five or six years old,
I was at the store with my mother and I saw this
little red truck. All of a sudden, I had an obsession
to steal that toy. I just had to have it, I don't know
if that's normal or not for a young kid to be
obsessed to steal something, but I remember
stealing that little red truck. It was a rush after I
had stolen it. I walked outside and I guess the toy

was bulging under my shirt. My mother asked me, "Boy! What is that you got under your shirt." My response was an elaborate lie, saying "The man in the store gave this truck to me," as I pulled out the stolen item. Mama marched me right back in the store and told the people I had taken something. She guaranteed her son would not do that sort of thing again. She took me home and gave me a good old-fashioned ass-whooping.

I was always trying to prove myself to other people, that's why my addiction was but a symptom of my disease. I was a thief, a liar and a cheat before I ever picked up a drink or a drug. My environment and poverty played a significant role in my drug addiction. My family lived right in the middle of the ghetto, on Clifton Street, which is one block from the infamous Cottonwood Road, in Bakersfield.

It was an area where I could look out of my back door and see the Street Life; lit up, live and in living color. I could see ladies of the night, the evolution of prostitution—the oldest profession known to man. This little boy was marveled by big Cadillac cars that shined like diamonds, and well-

dressed black men that called themselves pimps.
In the midst of it all, I could see dope-dealers
peddling death in plastic baggies, matchboxes or
small balloons.

What I saw *fascinated* me.

Somehow, I wanted to be a part of that lifestyle.
Poverty was prevalent thoughout the ghetto, but in
my household I was confused because I'd see
families on television shows like *The Brady Bunch*,
Father Knows Best, and *I Love Lucy*. Then, I'd see
my father working his ass off at a bullshit, local
cotton compress job. I'd see him leave early in the
morning and get home late in the evening, always
struggling to pay the bills.

My brother, Leon, also had an influence in my
life at that time. He was five years older than me
and always very protective.   He loved me very
much like a lot of big brothers. He taught me how
to take my first steps as a toddler, showed me how
to swim, how to put my groove on before I ever
went to my first dance. He became one of my
heroes. He'd watch me in school and tried to stop
me from hanging around some of the bad kids. He
was my protector, my best friend, and he thought,

somehow, he could save me from the street life and the inevitable.

I was a young boy born with three disabilities. First, I was blind, and everybody thought I had a genetic illness of retina pigmentosis from my grandmother, my fathers' mother. But my mother was a prayer warrior, so her and my other grandmother, my mothers' mother, got together and prayed for my eyes to see. After that, I had adolescent arthritis, and there was a period of time when I couldn't walk. Again, my mother and grandmother prayed for my limbs to move and I walked again. Then, I had a speech impairment and, one more time, those two prayer warriors asked God to give me the ability to speak. Soon after, I began to have fluency with my words.

This little boy had another defect. That defect was my fascination for the streets.

I was always self-centered, self-seeking, spoiled and needed attention and appraisal. My ego always sought recognition. I could see others getting this recognition from people in the street life. So I began to identify with this ideal. The ideal of the streets, the fast life, was very attractive to me. I became charmed...hypnotized. The pimps, ho's, hustlers and dope-dealers became the magic in my life. The bright lights and the glitter of the streets became my destiny before I ever picked up a drink at the age of seven. I chased this ideal, the illusion of the street life—the fast life, fast money, fast women and the dope game—for over thirty years. I sought not God, not man, but this dream, this illusion. But every single time I ran after this dream, I'd find myself in an institution or a life and death situation.

In the second or third grade, my teacher asked me and other students to write something about one of our heroes in history. I wrote a literary piece on Louis Armstrong. To write such a brilliant piece, she said, was an unusual gift bestowed on one so young. Yes, I was a talented writer even then. I was also a child seeking attention and recognition. Since it wasn't feasible for me to get this attention in the normal, everyday life, my acting out always landed me in the Principal's Office for something or the other. My self-centeredness and ego would rear it's head, always wanting to be the big-shot...Mr. Popular...Mr. Big Stuff. There was a popular song at that time called Mr. Big Stuff. I envisioned myself as being this popular guy. That type of attitude followed me all through my school years.

I remember when my mother took me to vacation Bible school. She was a church going woman and she really wanted me in church. She thought, like my grandmother, that the church house could save me. Today, I'm grateful that my mother insisted on me going to church because that allowed me to at least know God. It set the spiritual base in my life now.

While in vacation Bible school, I had a cousin named Willie who was not only a cousin but he was like a second brother. My mother once said we were the loud-talkers of the family. We were always talking shit instead of listening to the teacher. She called us "Gibbs and Blibbs," which means we had a lot of mouth. But me an Willie always spoke what we felt. Willie went on to school when he got older and became a scholar. I, on the other hand, clung to the streets and always ended up in a jail or the penitentiary because of the criminal element that comes with drug addition.

My mother and father were extremely good
parents. My father, John Lindsay, worked on one
job for over thirty years. My mother was basically
a home-maker. When times got hard, and they
were always hard living in the ghetto, she'd work
out at one of the rich, white folks' house. She told
me one time, that at one of the houses she worked,
the lady's husband had made some type of
advances toward her. My mother, being very
religious and loving her husband and family more
than life itself, didn't even go back to pick up her
check. She said, "All money ain't good money"
and prayed for the lady's husband and family and
went on about her business.

As I went through school, the principal would
always be calling up my parents either for some
fight I started or for kissing some girl. I was
simply acting out, once again, because I needed
attention, praise and acceptance.

There was a time when a group of boys and
myself were on a mission to kill somebody. I was
about fourteen years old at the time. We were the
Westside football team. We had just finished
practicing at Sixth Street Park, which was in a

predominately black neighborhood. There was another team near by and they were white. Being a bully, I went up to one of the biggest white guys, and without a word, hit him dead in the mouth. I started throwing blow after blow across his head and face and the rest of my team jumped in swinging. The rest of the white team began to scurry down the street. We beat the young white boy and hospitalized him with major head injuries.

The police soon got involved and were looking for the assailants. When I heard the wire on the street about the police, every day was like walking on egg shells, but since I was the leader of the pack, I couldn't show any fear.

About a month later, I was at school doing my thing, which was mostly talking shit and trying to pick up on the girls. I was sitting in study hall, when I heard that the police were on the school grounds. They were picking up all the blacks that were involved in the beating. Suddenly, Bakersfield's finest walked through the doors of the study hall. When I looked up and saw the uniformed police, I almost pissed on myself. If someone had said, "Boo!" I think I would have jumped in mid-air. All I wanted to do was get up and run somewhere, but I knew if I did that I would only make things worse. So, I just sat there trying to be cool, while the teacher pointed me out to the police. I remember everybody and their mama's looking at me as the police marched me off campus and into the squad car. I found out that I was the last one to get picked up because the snitch feared that I would do something to him. I ended up in juvenile hall for the very first time.

Little did I know, but that would be the beginning of a vicious cycle. I would try to get attention which usually got me in trouble. My trouble would make me feel bad about myself. I would turn to drugs and alcohol to make myself feel better. As I got more involved with drugs and alcohol, it would inevitably send me to areas of my life I thought I'd never go. For the next thirty years, I would be in and out of institutions, just like that one.

A week later, we all went to juvenile court. Much to my surprise, the judge let me go home instead of sending me to Camp Owens Boys Home. My mother had Pastor Green, who was known all over California, come down and speak to the judge on my behalf. I think it was his words of prudence that made a big difference in my case. Most of the other boys were sent to Camp Owens.

I went back to school and started bragging on how I slipped between the cracks. The popularity that I had been seeking had come true. Now I was thought of as a gangsta that had been released. With this popularity came attention from the ladies, and that's when I met Marsha. She was the answer to all my prayers. Her skin was a brown, creme de menthe color, her eyes were dark but with a touch of magic that I felt when she looked at me. She was very shapely for so young but I think what really attracted me to her, was her incredible smile. I carried her books home from school, we had lunch together in the cafeteria, and many incredible walks through the park.

She was my Queen and I was her knight in shining armor. When I asked her to be my lady, Marsha was so fine that I thought she'd deny me. But, to my amazement, she said "Yes!" and I was off to the races. I loved that young lady with all my heart and I honestly thought we'd be together for life. I thought she was my soul-mate.

A few months later, however, our times together became less and less. There were no more lunches together, no more walks in the park. It seemed that she always had an excuse not to see me. One day, I got really drunk and made a complete fool of myself. This guy named Eddie was talking to her. When I went over to see what was happening, drunk off of some wine I had gotten earlier, she told me she was with someone else now. Damn! That hurt me real bad. I would've felt better if she had taken a gun and shot me dead. At least I wouldn't have to feel the pain. She might as well have spit in my face. I felt so bad and humiliated that all I wanted to do was lash out. So, I tried to start a fight with this dude Eddie. He was a little older than me and somehow he convinced me that real men didn't fight over women. I found out later that Eddie had been kick'n it with her all the time.

Marsha and I went our separate ways and I found out for the first time that love had a double-edge and it wasn't all that I thought it would be. Like the old saying, "You can't enjoy the fragrance of a rose without feeling the thorns it bears." It was "Stormy Monday" for me, for a few months. I had been hurt like I had never been hurt before. I hadn't a clue that this was part of growing up. It was a real hard time for me, and using drugs and alcohol made it seem easier. There was always alcohol when I couldn't get anything else. Alcohol was the mother-drug, I'd always start with a drink first.

I remember being seven years old when I was introduced to Gallo White Port wine. The alcohol had an effect like nothing I had ever experienced. I became a part of, rather than apart from. Alcohol made me feel like Superman. I thought no longer did I need anyone, anybody or anything. The pain of growing up and my need for attention and praise became an illusion. That first drink gave me instant gratification.

I would chase that illusion, that feeling, that euphoria, for many years before realizing that I had become a slave. That mother-drug took me on a vicious cycle of self-destruction. I was caught up in that predatorial, insidious disease of alcoholism and addiction. It would be countless treatment facilities, detoxes, psychologists, psychiatrists, jails, institutions and body bags before I would get tired enough to have the desire to get clean. It was then that I found God and the Twelve Steps that turned my life around.

After Marsha and I split up, my best friend, Reggie, hooked me up on the dope game. He and I sold weed all day long and made enough money to support our habits. I began using drugs like red devils, black beauties, whites and codeine. I then moved on to heroin, speed, cocaine and anything else I could get my hands on. Being a small-time dope dealer put me and my friend Reggie on a higher status. We had clout now, and we started kick'n it with older people, in particular, older women.

I met this older woman named Sheryl. She was the woman that introduced me to real hustling. She turned me out. She took this young, school boy and developed a man—or should I say a monster. Sheryl was the pearl and she rocked my world. She was absolute beauty in motion, golden brown with velvety-soft lips. She had eyes that told you that she was definitely number one.

Our romance wasn't like the everyday courtship. It was a relationship typically depicted in a Donald Goines book. Like the young man in the book Whoreson, I was drawn to the streets. My relationship with Sheryl became a "pimp and ho" situation. There were no candlelight dinners, no candy and flowers, no holding hands. We got caught up in the fast life. Sheryl took me on a journey of lust, drugs and money. She was a hooker by night and a dope-dealer by day. Her ex-man was doing life, and she had grown tired of not having a man. She told me she needed a man and a young man would fit the bill. She showed me how to make love to a woman. She let me know that my love making was worth dollars, especially as a youth. She'd sit me down and school me on the art of the pimp game. She told me if I wanted to be a good pimp, I had to pimp with a passion.

Once again, I felt acceptance in the street life. The pimps and the ho's, the awesome way I felt when this woman made love to me, and then to get paid, too. Man! I was on top of the world. Having this older woman straight out choose me, then take care of me, Damn! I was living in player's heaven and that was the icing on the cake. I thought I could do no wrong. I thought I was the shit.

I began to get violent with Sheryl. I was always trying to prove myself a real pimp, a real player. I knew that real pimps and players beat on their ho's. Still chasing my illusion, still using drugs and alcohol, it was just a matter of time and we eventually parted company.

For most of my life I laid in the gutter, looking down on the world. I never had a clue that drugs and alcohol were slowly killing me. Today, because of a lady called mama and by the grace of God, I don't have to live in that frightful, cesspool of addiction, anymore.

Chapter 7   **On a Mission...Cottonwood Road**

Cottonwood Road was the strip. It was like Filmore, Harlem, South Central, Watts, etc. It was like all these places, but most of all, it was hell in the ghetto. It was a place where pimps, players, hustlers and ho's would congregate. A place where dopefiends shot dope, once-ta-tutes became prostitutes, and crime was a daily affair. I was twenty-one years old and fresh out of Tracy, Gladiator School. Once again, I thought I had all the answers but what I really had was not a Damn thing. There I stood on the strip, Cottonwood Road, thinking how lucky I was to be with Wendy.

I took to the "street life" like a moth to a flame. The streets were hypnotizing . It was as if something were pulling me, as if something had taken over and was controlling my every move. It was 1971 and I had been out of prison all of one day. The brothers in Tracy were depending on me to carry the Black struggle to the streets.

I had made a solemn promise to my mother never to return to prison again. I had all the good intentions of keeping that promise as well as following through with the Black struggle. But the day I got out of prison, the bus stopped at a small, one-horse town with a liquor store. I went directly in the store and bought me a bottle. I figured with all the knowledge I had gained in prison, that I could have just one! But that one took me right back into the horrors of my addiction.

When I made it home to Bakersfield that evening, I talked to my mother. We talked for a while as my father listened intently. He had always been a good provider. He was a worker among workers, and worked every day for as long as I can remember. He was a member of a local union, and his job helped him pay the bills. When he wasn't working in the union, he'd pick in the cotton fields, the vineyards, or the orange groves, he'd cut roses, drive tractors or any other laborious job. He was an uneducated man in terms of schooling but he had common sense. He once told me, "If a man didn't have common sense, that education wasn't worth a dime." So that day he listened with my mother to all the good things I was going to do for my people.

I was expressing how the system had done us. I would quote Malcolm X, Mao-tse-tung and other revolutionaries, and talk about how I was going to follow these revolutionaries and help save the world. It was really kind of funny, because all the time I was talking about the things I was going to do, I'd go into the bathroom at intervals and take a drink. Then, right on cue, I'd come out speaking again. Going on about how I had changed and the difference I was going to make in the world. My father was a wise old man and he would smile, saying something encouraging like, "Right On! Right On!"

My father, John Lindsay, was an alcoholic but I never saw him drink because he stopped drinking when he was twenty years old. Once, he told me that something devastating had happened to him when he had gotten drunk. He said he used to carry two guns. One night, back in Oklahoma, he drunkenly shot his guns aimlessly in the air. When he woke up the next morning, he realized that one of his bullets had actually creased his mothers hair—Grandma Lindsay. From that day on, until the day he died at the age of 72, he never took another drink. I believe that my father had a spiritual awakening. That traumatic experience caused something in him to change.

My father would often tell me, "If you could only leave the drugs and alcohol alone, one day you could make something of yourself." He always had high hopes for me. He used to tell me stories about the old times back in Oklahoma. He said there were times when things were extremely hard. On a good day, sometimes, he would make twenty-five cents. Most of the time there wasn't enough food to go around. In the winter months, the thunder storms would make so much noise that he and his brother, Jimmy, would go up to the white owners' house and steal a pig or two and bury them, to retrieve at a later time. His family lived in a cave because there wasn't enough money to live in a house.

He was looked up to by the rest of the family. He was the first to leave Oklahoma for California. He got a job chopping cotton, built him a tent on the farm land, and saved his money. Then he went back to Oklahoma to get the rest of the family. He was a good man and never hit my mother in the 35

years they were married. Even though my father
wasn't alive to see me turn my life around, I
believe that somehow, spiritually, he knows I'm
living my dream today.

Later that night, my brother Leon picked me up
and we proceeded to "Party hardy!" I met a girl
named Wendy that said she liked my style. She
gave me a few red devils and followed my lead
about the revolution. Before the night was over,
we were screaming revolution and taking more
pills. Wendy was my first piece since I had been
released, so automatically, I fell head-over-heels in
the fantasy of love.

There I stood on the strip, Cottonwood Road,
thinking how lucky I was to be with Wendy. I was
still on top of my game because I had a few dollars
in my pocket, which to me proved I wasn't an
addict. I was as sharp as any of the other so-called
players on the block. Which, at that time, was the
proof in the pudding that I had my shit together.

When I got through standing on the strip, letting
everybody know that I was back in town, I caught
a ride to the nearest dope house and copped some
real dope. I copped a bag of heroin and went back

to my new lady's house. When I got there, the house was packed and people were partying their asses off. I grabbed Wendy's arm and took her to the bathroom with me. I showed her the bag of heroin and all she could say was, "Can I have some?" So we proceeded to fix, as I shot mine I watched her from the corner of my eye, and could tell she had been using for a while. There were ugly track marks on her arms and hands which made her hard to hit. When I finished fixing, in a semi-nod, I noticed her pulling her tight pants down. She didn't have any panties on but there was no embarrassment about her nudity. What was on her mind solely, was getting the drugs in her body. She had this one spot right next to her pubic mound, which was a mass of black hair. Wendy was a fine, black woman that stood about five-foot-seven. She had soft, brown skin and sable eyes that seemed to reach out and touch you. "Mmmmm..." she muttered as she made a direct hit. "This is some good dope, baby. I hope I don't O.D. because I had a few pills this morning."

No, she didn't overdose, but she came real close. I had to walk her around for about an hour before she got herself together. She was real grateful that I was there for her. I don't know why I didn't go out like a light. I guess because I had a little common sense and wasn't too greedy. I also knew my system was clean because of my abstinence while I was locked up.

It was almost summer-time and the sun played tag on the moving clouds. I had been home a couple of months. Wendy and I had started arguing everyday. One night, this dude came over named Wally. I had gone to the store to get a couple of bottles of wine. When I got back I heard loud screams in the bedroom. When I opened the bedroom door, Wally had Wendy spread-eagle. His pants were down below his knees and he was asshole and elbows. My first reaction was to kill this motherfucker, so I took one of the bottles out of the bag and proceeded to put some choice licks upside this brothers head. The first or second lick should have done the trick because blood shot everywhere. But he still continued to rape Wendy, so I continued to put wear and tear on this nigga's head until he finally screamed. The screams didn't seem to be from the beating I was putting on him.

No! He was screaming because he busted a nut. "Damn!" I thought, "This has got to be the freak of the week." Incredibly, he suddenly jumped up and began to run, and as he ran, he literally ran over my little ass. He was a big, corn-fed brother, about six-foot-six, and weighed around three-hundred pounds. There I was, watching this big, black brother, bare-ass naked running out the door, holding his private parts.

I had been spending a lot of time on Cottonwood Road. I was always trying to hit a lick somewhere and the dopeman was always around any corner. I was living a real crazy lifestyle. I had been taking red devils and drinking Silver Satin wine with lemon Kool-Aid. I was dressed to impress, wearing a white-on-white, shark skin suit with a big, white hat tilted ace-deuce on my head. Before I knew anything, I was fighting this guy name Gino. He was a big fat dude, but he was built like a miniature tank. He was also known as one of the biggest dope dealers in Bakersfield. Sixth Street Park was where the fight started. It was a park where Blacks mingled at that time and on Sundays everybody used to let their hair down.

Sometimes it would get extremely dangerous over there.

This particular day, I was sitting on a park bench when this brother Gino came over and emptied a half a jar of red devils on the table. There were several young ladies that followed in his wake, like moths to a bright light. It was always that way—when you had the dope, you had the girls. So, me being loaded and having the nerve of a gun fighter, I decided I'd take a few pills for myself, not bothering to ask anyone's permission. The next thing I knew, I was being hit with this large fist. Suddenly, my small world came tumbling down around me. I really didn't know any better, because the drugs told me it was all right to do that kind of shit. There I was, stumbling through the park with this nigga whooping on my ass—hat knocked to the curb, and ass out trying to dodge the heavy blows. Gino whooped me from one side of the park to the other. Blood was all over and not a friend in sight.

Fortunately, when I reached the street I recognized a van my so-called friend "Big V" was driving. When I got to the van I saw a small

hatchet just behind the drivers seat. When I
reached into the van to get the hatchet, my so-
called friend Big V, pushed me in the other
direction. Here I was getting the shit beat out of
me, and this brother who I thought was my partner,
does something like this. I really didn't know what
to do. Then, miraculously, one of my aunts drove
by. We recognized each other at the same time,
and the car slowed and the door opened. When I
got in the car, I said "Damn! That was a close call.
Thank you, God, for getting me out of that one."
As we drove away she said, "You need to stop this
foolishness, because it's clear you're committing
suicide. It won't be long before the white folks
will be calling your mother, telling her you're
dead."

I had my aunt drive me back to the strip,
Cottownwood Road. I figured I'd go up there and
get me a gun or something, then go back and blow
the back of Gino's head off. But I was so loaded, I
could hardly stand up. When I got there, I ran into
another situation. A dice game was going on
beside Blackie's Liquor store. Blackie's Liquor
store was where all the night people hung out. A

partner of mine named Snookey was throwing the dice. Snookey was winning all this older man's money. The older brother had gotten mad at Snookey and pulled a knife. Snookey, being known as a gangster of sorts, pulled a small-caliber pistol and tried to fire but the gun didn't go off. He kind of smiled this shit-eating grin firing the pistol again. This time, the bullet hit its mark. The older man fell to the ground and shook for a moment and I never seen him get up again. An alarm went off in my head telling me I needed to get somewhere. Snookey took off first and I took off right after him, but I had sense enough to go in the other direction.

I heard later that Snookey was picked up for manslaughter and did three years for killing that brother.

That night, I ended up at a dopehouse on Williams Street, which was about six blocks from Cottonwood Road. I had run into a dope dealer friend of mine named Big Mike. He turned me on to some heroin that had been knocking people out. I thought that was just what I needed. It wasn't long before I fell out right in the middle of the floor. Some veteran dopefiends put me under a cold shower, put ice on my private parts and shot salt water in my veins. Pretty soon, I started to come around.

I realized just how close I had come to dying...but I wanted more.

About three days later, still on a suicidal mission—shooting drugs, taking pills, and drinking alcohol—I had grown tired and my body was telling me I needed to rest. I was still wearing the same white-on-white, shark skin suit that I had on at the park. My lip was busted and there were big ugly knots upside my head and blood stains all over my clothes. With the help of one of my homeboys, I got to my mother's house. I slept off and on for a week. After I rested up at my mother's house, I was right back on some corner trying to prove that I wasn't a punk.

In those days of my addiction, if it wasn't for my mother's house, the jailhouses, the penitentiaries, the detox centers, the treatment centers and the hospital beds, I would have been dead years ago. I was like a mad dog, that never understood why I was so mad.

I felt that the street life owed me something. I thought I had to be good to the game, so the game would be good to me. That's all I knew at that time, and to be quite frank, that's all I wanted to know. My actions were in accordance to my environment, and my environment consisted of pimps, players, hustlers and ho's. My role models were the people that got out there on the street and took what they wanted. It was the illusion of the hip, slick and cool—the pimps that made the ho's bow down, the immaculate players that drove fine cars, the ever-present hustlers and dope dealers, displaying their diamond rings to show their game was tight. It wasn't about being a doctor, lawyer, teacher or preacher. I was caught up in the lifestyle where education didn't matter. The only thing you had to do was survive.

My life was always dramatized by drugs and alcohol. From a young kid until my mid-forties, I was in and out of jails and institutions. As I write this book, I know that I'm on a different mission, and that mission is to carry a vision of hope...

Chapter 8   **The Angel of Death**

In my lifetime, I've done a lot of drugs from alcohol and pills to heroin and cocaine. If you could shoot it, toot it, drink it, inhale it, transmit it or eat it, I took it. But for me, I think crack cocaine was the straw that broke the camels back. Even though I had smoked crack off and on for years, it seemed that in the early nineties this drug took its toll on me.

It was after drugs had whooped me damn near to the curb in Fresno, that I decided to come to Portland, Oregon. My brother Leon moved to Portland years ago. He had gotten him a job working for the Tri-Met bus company. He bought a house, a car, got married and had a family. He always wanted to help me and for years he tried. So, I called my brother and asked for help. He told me that he would assist me in any way he could. But once I got to Portland, I got right back into my addiction.

I had been to Portland many times before, but this time I had reached the crossroads. I had been in Portland living with my brother when he got seriously ill. The doctor told me that my brother had cancer. He said that he had only a few months to live. I was devastated to hear the news first hand from the doctor. It brought me and my brother closer than we ever had been before. I cleaned up for a while, two or three days here and there, until my brother passed on.

Without my brother in my life to help me it made my life really hard. I could no longer rely on my big brother. He was dead, and I was so very sorry about it. But my disease of addiction wouldn't let up on me. The beast had become even more hungry and all it knew to do was eat at my soul. All it knew to do was to feed on my very existence. It fed on every area of my life. It became my everything.

It was 1993 when I hit a place in my addiction where I fell into a pitiful, incomprehensible state of mind, body and soul. I had reached a place of seemingly no return, a God-forsaken pit, a vicious cycle that would run me straight to the gates of hell. I believe that crack cocaine took me to my knees faster than any other drug I had ever experienced.

   Yes, Crack Cocaine was the "Angel of Death" and in the following words I express just how devastating that drug was...

Like the Recipe, for T.N.T...!
a terrible thang on the mind,
like Full Blown A.I.D.S.
of the most deadly kind...

At first it was powder, as white as snow;
a luxury extravaganza, a toot or a blow,
you could take it, shake it, or just leave it alone;
drink Mad Dog, Hennessey or Dom Perignon...

But the Day would come, "the Birth of Crack!"
and young school-girls would be tweek'n,
freak'n and Ho'n on the track;
unthinking times with so much pain,
and then the Revolutionized, micro-waved,
insidious cocaine!

From Business suites, to Prostitutes!
Beverly Hills to Beverly Manor,
when you hit that Glass Pipe;
don't a "Damn Thang" matter...!

Captain Kirk took you where no man had gone before;
but that Glass Pipe will take you even further and so much
more,
I'll make little boys forget their toys;
It'll make baby girls think they're boys...

The "Angel of Death," this Crack Cocaine!
It'll even make a scholar forget his name,
this Drug will make you dine with the swine;
It'll reduce you to the animal level,
It'll Blow your mind...

It was right before Christmas, and eerie snowflakes covered the dark streets as I put the last hit of dope upon the glass pipe. The fire from the overused lighter burned a bright orange and I could hear the crackling sizzle in its wake, as I inhaled the lady in the glass. As the drug began to work its powerful magic, I, for the first time in my life, could actually see a cloud of broken dreams. There was no more joy, no more good times and happiness was just an illusion. The world I lived in was in shambles, and the only thing I felt now, was incredible guilt and shame.

I sat there and watched the smoke. I could see marriages ruined, homes, apartments, clothes and fine cars, sold to the highest bidders. Children taken away and self-respect literally blown up in smoke. Then, finally, I could see a wise old lady, my grandmother, looking down on me. Shaking her head in wonder and despair, she wiped her tear-stained face from the years of pain that I had taken her through. "Damn!" I screamed, "I've got to quit this shit... this is going to be the last time, I swear it!"

A lady friend, who was pregnant with my baby,

and I were staying at this old man's house. It was more like a dungeon than a house. There was no electricity, no hot and cold running water, and the plumbing wasn't working because the water bill hadn't been paid in years. There was an overwhelming odor from those who didn't take the time to go outside to relieve themselves. There were rats almost the size of tiny children. They would travel mostly at night to feast on any prey at hand. In the evenings, the fire place would burn wood that the old man would bring in daily. It was real important to keep the fire going, especially at night, because in the night hours the rats became predators and it was open season for anybody that wasn't close to the fire. Sometimes, when we ate, we would cook our food in these big pots. The pots had to be secured with iron tops, because the rats would really get aggressive if there was any chance of them getting there eat on. It seemed at night that these rodents got bolder because they traveled in packs. One night, after everybody was asleep, I could see the rats actually copulating—having sex. This was a common occurrence in this house of horrors, this place of broken dreams.

Looking around at my surroundings, a hand tapped me on the shoulder, asking me to pass the pipe. I passed the pipe to my woman and said to no one in particular, "I've got to be the biggest fool in the world." I had begun to get real angry with myself earlier that day. The anger was because of a call I had made to my mother. I had begged my poor mother out of her last dollar. She had been saving her money for something special, a church function. I had lied to my mother, telling her that some people threatened to kill me because of some money I owed them. I told her I had to pay these people or she would read about my death in the obituaries. But, what was so cold about my situation at the time, was that I really had good intentions. I was going to buy some food for the house, pay the old man for staying there, and get enough dope to come up. I was going to control my addiction this time. But one more time, I became my best customer. A few hours after I picked up the money at the Western Union, there still wasn't any food, the old man hadn't received a dime, and I had spent all the money on crack cocaine. I was so broke I didn't have eye water to cry with.

The next day, I decided to go into treatment. It was a 21-day program that I had been through before, but this time I felt like I was ready to change. This particular treatment center was a very intensive inpatient facility. I believe in the old-saying, when the student is ready, the teacher will appear. I just wasn't ready at that time for the teacher to appear. I kept thinking I had all the answers, but in reality, I never knew the question. I never had a clue that just maybe, I had run out of answers. At the treatment center, I would sit in groups sometimes always knowing what to say and how to say it, but I never knew how to apply the things they suggested to me. I could always talk the talk, but I could never walk the walk.

I would start to have hope, I would start believing in what they were saying, but when it came to the acid test as far as applying recovery to my life, I'd come up short. I wasn't willing to put in the foot work. The counselors would say things like, "*Work the twelve steps*," "*Go to meetings*" and "*Find a sponsor.*" I could talk twelve-step stuff but I still didn't believe I was as bad off as the others. I'd even go to these meetings where they talked about ways to stay clean. But, like a friend of mine named Ricky P. would say, "I went for the P.O., the S.O. and the so in so." I wasn't really listening to the message. I would look for the differences in others instead of the similarities. Sometimes, I'd even find a sponsor that would help me in my recovery. But I'd never follow through, and consequently, I'd always end up blaming others when I found myself loaded again.

After 21 days had passed in treatment, I graduated from the program and I really felt that I could make it this time. I felt that all the pegs were in place and the pieces of the puzzle were finally coming together. To prove that I was serious, my first day out of treatment I went to a twelve-step meeting and continued to go on a regular basis. But there was something missing because right around thirty days of sobriety, I started thinking about the old-saying, "Once an addict always an addict."

I know there was one thing I had always done wrong. Once I got clean and started feeling better about myself, I always thought I was strong enough to start hanging around old friends. I thought I owed it to them to show everybody that I was staying clean. The lady friend that was pregnant with my baby at the time, was still using and everybody and their mama had told me to leave her alone. But they didn't understand that I was in love and I thought that if my woman would just follow my lead, she and I could stay clean and serene and live happily ever after. I really thought I could put on this red cape, and like superman, save her. But once again, I came up short on the stick.

I needed to realize that I could only save one person and that was myself. It was still the "mystery of 1993," as I call it. My lady and I had our baby and soon after the authorities took the child because it was born addicted. We had been on a mission for awhile and we both woke up dope-sick in a motel room somewhere on an Interstate Highway. It was the second day of the month. We had partied the night before like nothing else mattered because we both had received money from the County and State. We had about twenty dollars between the both of us, and it was just about check-out time at the motel.

Suddenly, I got this ingenious idea to call the
dopeman to get a wake up. There I was, I didn't
have any place to stay, no food to eat and the only
thing on my mind was getting a hit of dope.

I made the call and the connection came by.
Since I was such a good customer he gave me a
double up for my money. After we got our flight,
being good and loaded, we walked up to the corner
store where I proceeded to steal a bottle of
Thunderbird wine. Every time I smoked crack
cocaine I'd get over-amped. I couldn't afford a bag
of heroin to mellow me out, so the next best thing
was alcohol.

After drinking the wine, I started acting a fool.
While standing on the corner of Interstate and
Lombard waiting on the bus, I started flirting with
every woman I would see and cursing out people I
didn't even know.   Then I decided to focus on my
next move. I thought about dropping my boosting
hand at one of the major department stores at the
Lloyd Center mall. It was early afternoon when I
stepped off the bus at the shopping center. My
lady and I had a routine—we would go in as a
couple and she would check the prices of the

merchandise as well as watch my back. She would put her hand on the items I was to steal and I would very smoothly snatch the clothing off the rack and stuff it in such a way that one couldn't detect the bulk underneath my clothes. We had been doing this for quite a while and my confidence was always restored when I would walk out of the store undetected.

With the merchandise intact, my lady and I were off to the races. When we got back on the Northeast side of town, we ran into this brother that called himself Red-Bone. We sold most of the merchandise to him for cash, which was rare, because most drug dealers would much rather give you drugs for the merchandise. But I knew this brother pretty good, and I needed some heroin to go with the crack cocaine, so I convinced him we had to have cash money.

It was a series of vicious cycles. We would go out everyday and steal, beg and borrow. Cop the dope from the dopeman and get a room in a flea-bit motel. Lord only knows how very badly I wanted to stop this cycle but every morning I would come to and hear that familiar knock on the door for check out time. I knew I wasn't ready yet and was going to be doing this until I hit some kind of bottom—or died. I always thought that I would die with a spike in my arm or a crack pipe in my mouth. I was so overwhelmed in the insidious web of addiction that no amount of human aid could help me. I was suffering from a hopeless state of mind, body and soul.

It was about this time that God made a divine intervention in my life. I had just made another move on one of the local shopping malls. I didn't know it then, but one of the floor-walkers had been checking me out for the last month or so. I had just pulled a whole rack of children's clothes off the hangers, stuffed them under my coat and was on my way to the exit when three of the biggest security guards I had ever seen grabbed me by both arms. They lifted me in mid-air and every thing but Clothes-R-Us fell out on the floor. In a way, I was kind of thankful because I knew eventually someone was going to kill me.

I was sent to the Multnomah County Jail with a couple of theft charges, a possession—because of some residue on a pipe—and I also had an old

warrant. I was in jail about a month. If I had been
in California, the only thing that would have beat
me to the penitentiary would've been the
headlights on the bus.

When I got out of jail, I got a nudge from the
Judge to go to this drug court program. Things
were going pretty good at first in this treatment
program. I would go to my groups, talk to my
counselor, take U.A.s regularly and I even started
going to a few twelve-step meetings again. As a
result, I was blessed with a nice house with a
picket fence, a good, part-time job and a car. My
life was good again and I thought I was really
doing recovery this time. Someone in recovery
once told me, "When you do the work, you get
paid and when you don't do the work, you don't
get paid." That was the bottom line.

I had stopped going to meetings and stopped
being involved in the program. One night, about
six o'clock in the evening, I had just gotten off
work and had walked through the door. My
significant other was in the bathroom. All of a
sudden, I felt something was wrong. There was a
distinct odor in the air. I had smoked crack long

enough to know the smell, so when my lady came out with her eyes bulging out of her head with the crack look, I knew she had been smoking. The first thing she did was start looking out the windows.

Crack makes most people have a paranoia to some extent. It's a speed that works on the nervous system in such a way that you can't stay still. You're always moving or picking up imaginary things on the floor. These are just some of the symptoms and they vary to different degrees.

I had about ninety days clean and sober. I was still detoxing from my drug addiction and my first reaction was anger. I wanted to put my foot in this woman's ass, but then, I said to myself, what's the use. If you can't beat them, join them. As a result, I went on a run for about six straight months. I was about a month into my addiction and I could no longer pay the rent or anything else. I knew that I was too hot in the shopping centers, so me and the dopeman made a deal that he and his crew could set up shop in my house as long as my needs were met. The rent would be paid and most of all, I would have enough dope to smoke.

After that it was..."On, like popcorn!" That was the beginning of the end. I allowed this brother that called himself Boo-Man to come in to my house with his crew and deal drugs. The street I lived on was predominately white. It was a quiet neighborhood, blue and white-collar workers that worked hard to keep their neighborhood up. On day-one that Boo-Man stepped in my house and started dealing, this quiet neighborhood drastically changed. The street lit up like little Las Vegas. It was like a circus of horrors, a carnival of dopefiends that would march endlessly on missions of hopelessness and complete despair. The people were parading day and night, always selling themselves to the highest bidder.

My house was wide-open like a corner 7-11 store, twenty-four hours a day. In the midst of it all, I would be sitting in the back bedroom of the house either pushing the pipe or putting another one up on the glass dick. As I did this, day after day, I would have freak shows with some of the ladies. These women would do almost anything for a hit of crack. There were times when Boo-Man would come in and give me a handful of rocks and the sky would be the limit on what I would have them doing. I would take advantage of the women, including my lady, in these vile, sexual festivities. Some of these women could have been movie stars or Queens in another life, but in the dopehouse they were slaves to my every whim as long as I had the dope. Boo-Man wasn't an addict himself but for some reason he liked my style. I think it was because of my past as a pimp and player from the old school. I would tell him elaborate stories about my hard-core pimping career.

You'd have to be familiar with the book, *Dopefiend* by Donald Goines, to get the best description of some of the things that went on in my house. Donald Goines, being the greatest ghetto writer ever known, is very descriptive about the animal levels that some of the women would go to get their drugs. Unlike the main character Porky, who never used drugs, I became my best customer. In about six months, I was on the streets—broke, penniless, hopeless, helpless and lost. My only choices were to go back to jail, treatment or kill my motherfuckin' self. I had become the wretched of the earth and I wanted to die.

Chapter 9   **I Didn't Have to Die**

It was summer, and rain fell on Northeast Portland as the sky seemed to hide its face from me. The whole damned world seemed to come down on my shoulders that day. I was pushing a Safeway cart with everything I owned in it. I hadn't bathed in weeks, my hair was so badly matted that I had sores on my head. I had messed and pissed on myself because I couldn't control my bowels. That morning, when I came to in a cocaine stupor, I started walking aimlessly down Martin Luther King, Jr. Blvd. People would shake their heads and start walking faster, trying their best to put some distance between me and them. So-called friends would drive by and laugh in my wake. School kids would point fingers and hold their noses as they passed me. It was one of the coldest days of my entire life.

The landlord, with a police escort, had put me out of the house. They stressed how bad they wanted us out, and "out of town by sundown," if possible. Like many other dope houses, we had been closed down. The rent had not been paid in months, and the police, working with the landlord and neighbors, finally put us on the street.

Incredibly, as I walked pushing the cart in front of me, I saw people that I thought less fortunate than me. Wine-heads and tramps lying out on the street reeking with urine and alcohol. I thought about the times when I'd say to myself, "If I ever got that bad, I'd kill myself." I don't know how long I walked but I must've been approaching Burnside Street. I started seeing a lot of the American Indians and Mexican Americans. I started to hear the old familiar terms spoken by Spanish dope dealers. "Coca! Cheeeva ...for sale!" I turned around and realized I had walked all the way down Martin Luther King, Jr. Blvd. I felt so bad, I was so tired of the pain and humiliation that I just wanted to find a hole and hide from the world.

I was always such a proud man, keeping my appearance up to par. Driving nice cars, wearing the best of clothes, living the good life. I just couldn't comprehend how my life could get so bad, so quick. I had come from a good family, a good home, had loving, caring and respectable parents. Why was this happening to me? I asked myself over and over again. Why me? Why me? I watched the other street people and saw a lady searching for food in a trash can. Another person wobbled across the street on crutches and there was this old guy sitting on the curb talking to himself.

I was on the corner of Burnside and MLK when this old man, looking as if he were a thousand years old and had been sleeping on the streets for years, approached me and said, "I remember when you had yourself together, but damn! Brother man, look at you now!" He passed me shaking his head. Suddenly, he turned around, and I realized that he couldn't see me, he was blind. Then he did something that really shook me up. He pointed at his unseeing eyes and said in a quiet voice, "Ain't nothing so bad it couldn't be worse." I remembered those were the same words my grandmother would say to me. "Ain't nothing so bad, it couldn't be worse."

I started crying like I never had in my life, right there on that corner. I cried ... and I cried ... and I cried! No matter how hard I tried to stop crying, I just couldn't stop. I don't remember how long I cried on the corner that day, but I started to understand what the old man's words meant. I began to understand what was going on in my life and why my life was in so much turmoil and pain.

I believe God speaks through people and I believe that old man brought me a message from my grandmother. Even though it would be a little longer before I found recovery and turned my life around, I believe that was some sort of spiritual awakening for me. Afterwards, I looked for that old man and it was as if he had disappeared into thin air, like an angel.

I pushed that Safeway cart with everything I owned out into the street and went into a nearby detox center, not looking back.

I had been to detox many times but I had been to this particular detox center more times than I could count. My first three days there were the hardest for me. I'd pray in the morning, go eat breakfast with the rest of the people, and then go to the groups. The groups didn't do a lot for me, but in the evenings, these volunteers would come in and share their experiences, strength and hope.

They would talk about the 12-steps, finding a God as they understood him, and powerlessness. They would say things like, "Keep it simple," "Let go and let God," and "Keep coming back." They would stress, "You don't have to stay sober the rest of your life, just for today! One Day at a Time ...!"

I had heard this stuff many times before, but this time I started to really "listen to learn and learn to listen." What was really interesting about these people was that they were just like me. They were alcoholics and addicts that were actually staying clean. What amazed me was, "they were talking my language." Some of them I had actually used with. We had been in our addiction together, so I knew they were serious about this thing called recovery.

Some nights, before I'd go to sleep, I'd think about some of the things I had heard from these people that were just like me. I'd say to myself, "If they can do it, just maybe, I can too?" The average stay for this detox center was five to seven days, but I stayed two weeks. I was really scared and I knew another relapse was right around the corner. When I got out, I went straight to a twelve-step meeting again. But for some reason, again, I couldn't stay clean. I believe I was three weeks sober, staying down town on Sixth Street. I was going to school and doing pretty good, when an old girlfriend came by one day that had been drinking. She was crying, telling me her problems with life issues and her situation with self-esteem. Of course, my heart went out to her. Having three weeks sobriety, my mind began to provide incredible reassurance, telling me I may not have a problem. Having three weeks clean proved that I wasn't as bad off as those other people. So, before she left, we were both drinking.

It was 1994 and once again I was in the depths of my disease. That drink with that old girlfriend unlocked the cage of *addictman*. I always thought I could get clean, but staying clean was another issue all together. I still had my apartment on Sixth Street, was going to school, and—amazingly enough—was keeping a few dollars in my pocket. I had moved this Mexican dope dealer, named Jose, in with me so once again, I didn't have to worry about my drug supply. Jose was a heroin dealer, which meant I had the best of two worlds. I'd got out and buy crack on the street and then mellow out on heroin. Once again, I thought I was in control.

Jose started to trust me from day-one he stepped into my apartment. He'd give me a certain amount to deal and we'd split the profit at the end of the day. If there was anything left, which there usually was, he'd let me have it. Unlike my house on the northeast side of town, we were exceptionally careful. First of all, I couldn't stand another bust because even though I never got thrown in jail, I knew the police had to be watching me. Also, we were very careful because of the area we lived in. The building that I was living in definitely wouldn't go for those all night parties I loved so well. Most of the people we dealt with would meet us on the street. Our clientele was a little different because we were dealing with mostly heroin addicts. Once again, it appeared that I was taking care of business successfully, and that I didn't have a problem with drugs.

Sometimes, Jose and me would be taking care of business on the street, making a delivery or something, and I'd see somebody from recovery.

One time, I was catching the bus and a good friend of mine named Bill was driving. Bill knew my brother, Leon, before he died. Bill would always have a good word for me. He would never look down on me. He'd say things like, "Keep on keeping on, Brother!" I'd shoot him some hip, slick and cool stuff back, telling him that "Everything was everything." But in reality, my head had taken out a contract on my ass. Even though I couldn't admit it at the time, every time I saw people that were living a clean and sober life, I wanted what they had. For most of my life, I thought I was in control. But someone once told me that I couldn't "think my way into better living." I had to "live my way into better thinking."

Jose and me had a good thing going for a while. We were making money and I was staying loaded. One night, I was laying up with one of my ladies, because I thought ladies go better with dope, and the phone rang. Jose had gotten busted on a drug-related charge, and didn't know when, or if at all, he'd be getting out. I hung the phone up, and suddenly, my body started to act up. I had a few bags, but that wouldn't last me but a few days. I had a real bad habit on heroin and I knew my bottom would soon be coming up to hit me dead in the face.

A week later, and I was as sick as two dogs. I had a dealer's habit, but there was no Jose and no dope. I knew I was going to have to do something, but what? I didn't want to go back into the shopping centers and start boosting again. A lot of the stores I couldn't go into anymore. I had reached a point in my life where I was "Tired of Being Sick and Tired!" I just didn't want to live the life I had been living anymore.

As I sat in my apartment, full of despair, I didn't know what road to choose. I was at a crossroads in my life and I knew I had to do something different. I had called my mother earlier that day in hopes that she would come to my rescue. But that little old lady was tired of my shit. She made it real clear to *leave her the fuck alone.* All my so-called friends made it their business to give me a lot of distance.

There I was with two choices: Did I want to *Live*, or did I want to *Die*? It was that simple.

God had put me in a position where I had to totally depend upon him. I was so very scared, frightened, confused, lost and alone. I had been throwing up all day, but for the very first time in my entire life, I believed that through God, and only God, there was hope for even a wretched, dopefiend like me.

Many years ago, my mother and grandmother told me that in the very darkest hours of pain that God would come to me and bring forth light to the darkness. Those wise old ladies also told me that "Prayer from the righteous avails much."

I fell on my knees and screamed a merciful prayer. "Please, God! If I haven't done too much wrong, Help Me!" I wanted so badly just to Come Home. Home for me was the grace of God, the 12-steps and recovery.

Somehow, I knew I didn't have to die.

Chapter 10 **Coming Home**

For most of my Life, the Streets I roamed;
Shot dope, drank wine, and
Suddenly, the world was gone; Coming Home...

False illusions, total confusion and
the Dice roll; snake-eyes.
A crack pipe,
And another Dead Soul; Coming Home...

Never waking up but always coming to;
laying in a rat hole, not knowing a Damn thang to do!
Wallowing in the gutter with unseeing eyes,
Dying a hundred deaths with no compromise...

Pain and suffering and the stakes were high;
trying to find a place, now, just to die...
then I ask 'Him' for a sign as I screamed and cried...!

Then God had a notion; a Miracle in motion,
and my Life would be Won,
like the Prodigal Son; Coming Home...

Being once blind but now I can see;
coming from a Spiritual Death,
to being all that I can be,
from jails and institutions which were my past;
to standing in the light of God... at last!

It was once said that I was dead but now I'm alive;
I walked through the miring fog but I survived,
and today I carry a message of hope;
instead of drugs... alcohol... and dope!

And although there's times when I feel alone;
I've surrendered to my Father, and he brought me home;
Coming Home...Coming home...I've Come Home...

After my prayer in my most darkest hour of pain, I believe that God directed my thinking. I walked to the bathroom, a free man with hope at last. I took off my clothes and got under the shower. As I showered, I continued to pray asking God to keep me sober. I could not, and would not, go back into my addiction but by the pure grace of God. When I got out of the shower, I rushed to put on my clothes. Something had happened that day. I felt for the first time in over thirty years of using and drinking that I could do this. I could stay clean.

I had an urgency of hope because something inside of me was driving me to a 12-step meeting. The feeling was so incredible, so immense, that I just couldn't get to a meeting fast enough. I rushed out the door and down the hallway to the elevators. The elevators weren't moving swiftly enough for me, so I took the stairs and literally ran down the ten flights. When I reached the street, the buses were moving to slow as well, so I began to run down Southwest Sixth Street like a crazy man. After I got to Washington and Sixth Street—I can't remember whether I had bus fare or not—the bus

driver must've seen the urgency on my face
because he allowed me on. I had two 12-step
books, so as I rode the bus to Northwest Portland, I
read things like, "How it Works," "Into Action,"
and "There is a Solution." There were people in
these books that seemed to know everything about
alcoholism and addiction.

When I made it to my destination, a big white
house that "sat on the end of the block," I knew
there was hope in those rooms for me. When I
entered the building, I ran down some steps that led
to a basement. I seated myself in one of the chairs
and could see people with smiles on their faces.
People with understanding and compassion that
knew from experience exactly what I was feeling.
They shook my hand and hugged me, telling me
they would "love me until I could love myself."
They talked about the 12-steps, sharing their
experiences, strength, and hope!

I'd been coming around 12-step programs for
years, but this was the first time I really heard what
they were saying. I'll never forget that evening,
July 24, 1995. As I sat there in that basement, I
heard people from all walks of life sharing. People

that had been given a reprieve on their lives. They were doctors, lawyers, teachers, preachers, skid row and street people that had arrived helpless and hopeless, and now, they were living good lives. What was so awesome about this fellowship was that I knew I belonged. I felt for the first time, a part of, rather than apart from. Before, where there was hopelessness and despair, now, I felt a sense of peace. I knew in my heart of hearts, that like the Prodigal Son, I had come home.

For over thirty years, I had lived a life of self-destruction. I had always blamed the other guy, my parents, my ex-wives, my children or the system we lived in. It was always the "Jones' next door," the judges, the prisons or the jailhouses. It was always somebody or anybody else's fault but my own, but that night in the basement of that house, I started to realize that I was to blame for all my troubles.

I listened to people speak at that 12-step meeting. I began to hear my story, my grief and my pain. There was a unique diversity but there was also a familiarity in the air that had depth and weight.

I had been sitting for about thirty minutes when this bearded gentleman named Michael L. stepped up to the podium. He had thirty-two years of sobriety at the time. There was something very special about him and how he spoke. He spoke with grace and absolute eloquence. When he spoke there was something mesmerizing about his words. He said things like "Easy does it," "First things first" and "Work the steps or Die." Most of all, what I heard that day that made all the sense in the world was when he, with blue eyes that seemed to shine, said "Faith without Works is Dead." Like a burning bush, Michael L.'s words inflamed as he spoke about how "Action... Action... and more Action" was the key to staying sober. He said he couldn't *"think his way into better living,"* he had to *"live his way into better thinking."*

There was magic in the room that evening, July 24, 1995. After he spoke, I felt the need to go up to the podium and share. I wanted to talk about the pain I was going through. I had heard somewhere in recovery, in those rooms, that if I talked about my feelings that somehow I would begin to feel better.

So, while the chairperson was speaking, I suddenly couldn't wait for him to finish what he was saying. I raised my hand to be recognized. I was desperate to relieve myself of my pain but he didn't recognize my hand. *With my hand still raised high, I got up out of my seat, shaking so badly that I could hardly stand, and walked up front.* When I made it to the podium, I said that I was dying inside and that I needed to share. His eyes spoke of understanding and he hugged me and sat back in his chair.

I can't even begin to comprehend or remember what happened or what I said that evening at the podium, but when I finished speaking, I felt amazingly better and had a sense of peace.

That night started a change in my life that was profound and unique. From that point on, I knew I was on a journey for the rest of my life. After the meeting, I walked up to that bearded gentleman, named Michael L., and I asked him to help me, to sponsor me. We must have talked for a couple of hours. He asked me if I was ready to go to any lengths to stay sober. I told him that I was as willing as the dying could be. When we finished talking, he shook my hand and hugged me, telling me to "keep coming back."

That night, I went to another meeting, and another meeting, and another meeting. I was too scared to be anywhere else but in those rooms of recovery. When I got home, it was after midnight. As soon as I walked through my apartment door, I fell on my knees and thanked God for keeping me sober that day. I didn't sleep well that night because I was detoxing from alcohol, heroin, cocaine, and methadone. But God was doing for me what I could not do for myself, and allowed me at least a few hours rest.

The next day, I went on something of a marathon. I went to meetings day and night. I was running after my recovery with a hope to die passion. I was doing my recovery like I did my drugs and alcohol. It was told to me that most people didn't make it, so I needed to do more than most. On this journey for my life, I was determined to "suit up and show up," otherwise, as some of the old timers in recovery said, "I'd be shootin' up and throwin' up."

Nothing else had ever worked for me and I

knew that if this recovery didn't work, I was going to be as "dead as the Graveyard." Many of my friends in their addiction had started dying. I heard that there was some bad dope in town. Some tar heroin had come out that year that was killing people I had known for years.

It was right before Thanksgiving Day of 1995, and I had four months of sobriety. I went to a funeral for a very good friend of mine, named Asmar. As I walked by his casket, I could see a reflection of myself. In him I could see my horrible lifetime of jails, institutions, dereliction and finally, death. His face was like a mask of incredible suffering and pain. As I looked at my friend's face, I could see searing images of dopehouses and crack dens. I could see blood-dripping arms, unattended children crawling on dirty floors and a sea of weary faces screaming for one last hit. In the midst of it all, there was a padded cell with no window on the door and an overwhelming darkness with an air of loneliness so morbid, so unbelievable, that my skin began to crawl.

At that precise moment, I became very grateful

for who I was because only by God's grace was
that not me lying dead in that casket.

During the funeral, friends and relatives were
walking up and offering words at Asmar's eulogy.
I stood up suddenly, walking to the front of the
church. I recited my poem entitled *The Last Days*.
Afterwards, when I got home and settled a bit, I
called my mother telling her I couldn't remember
certain events of my friend's funeral. I told her I
couldn't remember saying anything. She told me
not to worry about it because that was God
working through me. She said he was using me as
a vessel to carry a message. When I hung up the
phone, I got on my knees and thanked God that it
wasn't me in that casket. I prayed for my friend's
family, and those that were still suffering from the
disease of addiction. It took a few days for my
memory to come back and I became even more
grateful for that experience. It started to dawn on
me that life goes on, and that the addict that dies in
his addiction, lives through the hopes and dreams
of those that persevere.

By Christmas, I had gotten into service work
because, for must recovering addicts, the holidays

are very hard. My sponsor, Michael L., told me
that it would take me out of myself. In order to
keep my sobriety, I had to give it away. He also
told me, "Those that stay in the middle wouldn't
fall off the edge." I was certainty trying not to fall
off the edge because the edge, for me, was to fall
back into that insidious web of insanity.

When I was in that time of my life where I was
"Tired of Being Sick and Tired," I was suffering
from a Spiritual Death. A Spiritual Death is the
worst kind of death because you die from the
inside. I was at a point in my life where I was out
of answers. My answers would always take me to
the dopehouses, shit houses and penitentiaries.

So, whatever these recovering addicts and
alcoholics told me, I didn't question. I just
watched and did what they were doing. I simply
did what they did!

One of the most profound things I ever saw by
coming around the 12-Step Program, was this old-
timers birthday where he was celebrating *41 years*
of recovery. His name was Bob B. and they called
him the "Godfather" of the 12-Step Program.
What was important about Bob B. was the fact that

he's still doing the same things he did when he first got sober. He was still going to meetings on a regular basis, still working the 12-Steps, and still into service work. Ultimately, he was still clean and sober. I believe, like the pioneers, that recovery is not something that is over and done with. The 12-Steps are a never-ending journey for the rest of our lives, but you do it one day at a time. More importantly, you do your recovery *Just For Today.*

Recovery is not an event, it's a journey. It's not a project, it's a process.

Years ago, there was a gentleman named Reverend Ishmael Kimbrough that I befriended. He has been a big inspiration in my life. We were so much alike yet so different. We first met in the early eighties. He had moved from back east, bringing his family to California. He settled in Bakersfield where he built a church from the ground up. This man had the faith of a mustard seed and an urgency to help his brothers and sisters. He was a powerful man in his own right, and when he spoke, you definitely knew where he was coming from.

One day, when I was trying to stop drinking and using, he picked me up and took me to his house. We played dominos at his kitchen table. He told me something that has always stuck with me. He told me that *my soul was worth saving.* Sometimes, I'd be drunk as hell and he'd pick me up and take me to his house to eat and sober up. There was a time when this big speaking function was up at the police department. It was concerning police brutality in the Black community. I was half drunk, going back and forth to the bathroom sucking on a bottle of cheap wine. But this man named Kimbrough would only have words of encouragement for me. I would share my gift as a writer with him and he would tell me things like "God is one day going to use you to help people because you have a gift that a lot of people don't have." Reverend Kimbrough was that beacon of hope that I needed to help me make it to the other side.

Sometimes, I wish I could've turned my life around then, but like my grandmother would tell me, "You had to go through whatcha' had to go through, to get to where you're going." It's like some people told me in recovery, "*It takes what it takes to get us here and it takes what it takes to keep us here.*"

Right after Asmar's funeral came Christmas and New Year's and this time I didn't have to get loaded. I didn't have to bring the New Years in with a bang! This year, I wouldn't end up in a jailhouse, an outhouse, or overdosed in some alleyway.

My first year in recovery was the hardest but I went to a lot of meetings. People in recovery suggested 90 meetings in 90 days. I went to three outpatient drug treatment programs. I got into service work, which consisted of welcoming people that were new at the door, making coffee, secretarial work, chairing meetings, and anything else that recovery would suggest.

It was March 12, 1996 when I hit a place in my recovery where I thought God and the world had turned on me. I got a call from my mother that my dear grandmother had died and passed on. My Grandmother, like other grandmothers, was very, very special to me. We had a special relationship. It didn't make any difference how bad I thought my life was, she was always there for me. It didn't make any difference what jailhouse I was in, what penitentiary, or what hospital bed, she was always there for me. When my Grandmother died, I wrote these words for her entitled, *A Song for My Grandmother...*

For she was like a thousands shooting stars across the sky; and
Today we bow our heads with tears of Good-bye, a Guiding, so
special light,
ever sparkling... ever so bright!!!

Her smile had the love like no other,
unlike the love of my sisters or my brother,
for she had that so Special Magic, so many things was she...
but good or bad,
that Woman was Proud of Me...

And I can still remember that Wise Ol' Lady
when I was real small, just a baby...
Her eyes would sing songs of Joy...
And I can still hear her voice saying,
"You Go Boy!"

Many will say, she was before her own time, and her
Gifts of Life will always shine,
and it wasn't that many days, not long ago,
I would call her over the phone, just to Say Hello...

I often remember her sometimes in my Dreams, and in these
dreams we'd be in a prayer, she'd sing,
Oh... My Father!
If I should die, before I wake, I pray to God for my
Soul to take...

To me, she'll always be like a Mighty River, touching all with
Love...
And today, I sing a special song, just for her to take above...
Always and a day, I'll Love You like
no-other...
From me to You, A Song for My Grandmother.

I still have the pain of losing her, and I believe, spiritually, she looks down on me with a smile everyday. When my Grandmother died, I was devastated and I really didn't know if I could make it to the other side. I can't stress enough how painful her death was.

Soon after my grandmother's death, it was a day of sun, blue skies and pleasant warmth—a perfect day, but I was far from perfect. I could not explain the driving force that led me to the mossy concrete steps to the home of Marie Maul. Marie Maul was a special friend. In a sense, she was like my grandmother. She opened the door for me, offering the words, "Savon, your grandmother is in a better place now...she's in Heaven."

Like my grandmother, Marie was very religious. There was no Mountain high enough and no river deep enough to leave any question unanswered. She was a special lady, Marie Maul.

She offered her hand to me. I grasped it and we both kneeled in prayer. I was seized with overwhelming grief and unbearable pain. Then, at that moment, the grief and pain subsided—*she had annointed my head with holy oil.*

Soon after, she gave me the gift of the following words, "Savon, there is no problem big enough that God cannot handle, just walk with Him."

Later, I found myself wandering aimlessly through the Hollywood District of Portland in a three-piece suit. Suddenly, the pain of losing her became overwhelming and even greater than before. I was at the Hollywood bus transit center and realized I'd never see her again. The pain was piercing, agonizing, and totally heartbreaking. It was like something or someone had literally torn my soul apart. I looked at all the people standing around waiting on their buses. I looked at the sea of faces out there at the bus mall. I envisioned dope-dealers and the practicing addicts calling my name. I wanted to medicate my feelings and use so very bad! Then, like an incredible image, I could see those rooms of recovery. I could hear people, like my sponsor Michael L., telling me that there would come a time when no amount of human aid could help me. There would come a time when I would have to find a power greater than myself, and that power had to come from God.

There I was, at the end of my rope and I knew I had to humble myself to God. At that very moment, I knew I couldn't just stand there and pray. I knew I needed to be on my knees in order for God to help me walk through this. I said to myself, "What would all these people think if they saw me on my knees?" They would think that I was crazy or something.

You have to understand how great the pain was and how desperate I was for God to help me. I knew in my heart of hearts, that if I went back into my addiction, I would surely die. If not a physical death, I would be like the walking dead, my spirit would be lost forever.

So, I positioned myself between these two bus shelters, then closed my eyes and fell on my knees. I whispered to God to please help me because I couldn't do this on my own. I had on a three-piece suit, but none of that mattered. The only thing that mattered was for God to allow me to walk to the other side of my pain.

In the scriptures it says that God has wonders to perform. Just like magic, a miracle appeared, because as soon as I got up off my knees, the number twelve bus stopped right in front of me. I began to cry tears of gratitude, thanking God for doing for me what I could not do for myself.

I rode that bus to a meeting right off 12th and Sandy Boulevard. What makes the fellowship of the 12-step program so awesome, is the fact that no matter where you go in the world there are people, fellow addicts and alcoholics, that will reach out and help you. When I walked into that meeting that day, in tears and sorrow, I began to share my loss and my pain. There were people in that meeting that I had never seen before that walked up to me with hugs and understanding hearts. They gave me something priceless and unique that I'll never forget. Once again, I knew I had come home.

My mother told me, that for about three days she was very frightened for me. She said she didn't know whether I would be able to stay sober through the tragedy of my Grandmother's death. So, for three days, she prayed for me continuously. After the third day, she said that *she heard something in my voice that let her know that I was still standing on the mountain top, that I was still free.*

I didn't get a chance to go to my grandmother's funeral for many different reasons. But my mother told me later that my spirit was there. One of my grandmother's greatest dreams was to be able to see me turn my life around. For that, I am truly grateful because years have passed since then. I was only able to go through the pain of my grandmothers' death because God and the fellowship of the 12-step program let me know that I could walk through anything and make it to the other side.

It's my solemn, undying hope that those who read this book, will realize that there are dreams for those who have lost their dreams. They will realize that there is hope for those that are hopeless.

And for those that don't believe in Miracles, believe that Miracles still exist, because *My Naked Soul*, is a Miracle in itself.

Michael L., my friend and sponsor, were together at Reflections Bookstore in March, 1998 when Eldridge Cleaver, author of National Bestseller Soul on Ice, *came to Portland. We heard him speak and were there for his book signing.*

Bob B. is one of the pioneers of the 12-step program. Some call him the Godfather of Recovery. A humble, gentleman, he is a friend and one of my champions and rolemodels.

On the left, Romero, a friend with extraordinary taste and a motion in his step that lets you know he's real. On the right, my little brother Leroy, with his explosive nature and electrifying personality, who just fathered twins.

Joe Redcliff

Like a surging wind;
something deep within,
a modest, compelling man;
Joe Redcliff, my brother...my friend...

I remember when we first met,
down on the block, up on the set,
shoot'n, toot'n and drinkin' wine and Kool-aid,
talking about the ho's we laid...

We kicked game around the world!
tossed up a few of those tender-rony girls,
but he and I would soon discover;
that drugs and alcohol would become our friend and lover...

And even though we were brothers to the end;
the dope-life would become our ultimate sin,
and we'd end up in jails and institutions,
stagnating through the pain, trying to find a solution.

And one day we'd come up out of a nod;
and find a man we'd choose to call God,
and now we work, struggle and strive,
keeping God and Recovery alive.

So I thank you, brother and partner to the end,
Joe Redcliff, my brother, my friend!

There's an old saying, when one person dies another person takes his place. My son, Tyroby, a beautiful child that I love and cherish, was born right after his grandfather, my father, died in 1984. I'm so grateful because even though I lost a father, I gained a son.

When I first saw my little girl, Tequella, I knew that God was still in the blessing business. Even though I haven't had the privilege to see my daughter or son for quite a while, I love them both with all my heart and their beautiful mother Cynthia.

Eldridge Cleaver at a celebrated time at Reflections Bookstore. Eldridge signed one of his books, National Bestseller Soul on Ice, *and I had a chance to talk with him about my latest book* My Naked Soul. *We met twice that day, and on our last meeting he endorsed my books* The Soul of an Addict, Tired of Being Sick and Tired, *and* My Naked Soul. *Shortly after this photo was taken, Eldridge passed away.*

I'll always be grateful to my brother Eldridge for his support at that time, and for his spirit for human rights when he was Minister of Information for the Black Panther Party. He will always be in my thoughts and prayers, my brother, Eldridge Cleaver...

Grateful Acknowledgments

From the very essence of my soul this book was spawned. But if it hadn't been for God and the support and genuine love of certain people, this book, My Naked Soul, would be just an idea, a fleeting thought, a dream that I've had since childhood thrown into the mists forever. But because of these people and many others in my life, this dream has become a reality.

First, my sponsor, mentor and friend, Michael Lowell, who gave me his intuitive hope when I thought I couldn't go on. Then there was Joe Redcliff, my partner and best friend who showed me that I could always do better if I continued to work at it. Ricky Patterson, a dear friend that ignited my inspiration with his fiery dedication. Harrison D., I'd like to thank him for his humor and letting me know that he believed in me from the very start. Bob B., who I like to call "The Godfather of Recovery," I'd like to give a special thanks for his humility and profound wisdom and also for that light that seemingly always shines in his eyes that can only be described as absolute magic. I'd like to thank Lenita R. for her spicy, lady-like style and her heart-felt compassion as a person. Marih A. for her so sophisticated sensitivity and explosive mannerism that only real ladies possess. And of course, Jason Reynolds for his rare expression, explosive wit, and the time he took to cultivate my ideas and make them real. Andrew Scott for his brilliant perception and his unique ability to say exactly what I needed to hear. Bryan Pollard, a young man with extraordinary expertise, a man with electrifying zeal—a man with enough magic to make this book possible. My personal thanks to you, Bryan.

Street roots of Portland, I'd like to thank you for your immense contribution to our struggle against homelessness. Your gift to our community shines with intensity all over the world. D&P Printing, Tom and Leslie thanks for your invaluable help. Beverly Cartwright, a dear friend that passed away but her humor still makes me laugh. Tim Fontaine, thank you, brother, for being that helping hand in my time of need. Monica Lindsey, I can't say enough about our friendship and her fascinating energy to persevere. Most of all, I want to thank her for just being there for me in my time of need. Robert K., who once told me that my job was much more than just being a writer, he said my job was "the vocation of carrying the message of recovery." Gwen Harvey, who gave me a new look into the sparkling images of all black women. Belinda Oliver I'd like to thank for her dynamic determination in the art of poetry and her genuine sisterly love when I needed it. Terry J. for her words of encouragement and in particular the incredible excitement of her experience, strength and hope. Keith Dean, a friend that I reached out to and was never denied support. I'd also like to thank him for his seemingly electrifying humility that speaks through the quality of his style. Ronda Solomon, a woman in her own right, a lady with enough energy to inspire my dreams and let me know that my work was a gift to be shared. Elizabeth W., a real and dear friend that gave me some direction when I was still in a fog. Fred Kennedy, a brother that has a motion in his step that puts him in a category of his own, but a pureness of heart that showed me that the sky was the limit if I just believed in myself. Steve S., a gentleman that always speaks from the heart and helped me like no one else could and that was through

his own experience. Paul Knauls, Jr., a friend that
believed in my writing ability years ago and through
his dedication as an artist, he enabled me to see my
own potential. Jerry Duckett, a brother true to the
form, a man destined for success, a dear friend that
gave me his support and immeasurable hope. Mark H.,
a young man with zeal unexplainable and, because of
his determination to persevere, the help to carry my
potential. Terrie Coleman Lindsay I'd like to thank for
honesty, open-mindedness and willingness. Rebecca
Tavies for being my other mom and "stick'n to the
script." Robert Sollars was like a light at the end of the
tunnel when my vision was blurred, because of his
support and expertise I was able to go on. Monica
King, my favorite niece (even though sometimes she
doesn't think so) and my brother's oldest daughter,
through her I get a chance to see the love of my brother
Leon. I love you girl. Charlie Nanos, I thank you
brother for your incredible magic-like gift, and God for
bringing you in my life. My prayers are always with
you.

   Clifford Lewis, a coming-up artist that expresses his
talent through his brilliant and sheer immaculate
paintings, a dear friend and colleague that, because of
his brilliance, made me see my own. Terrol Johnson
I'd like to thank for his business-like style and
encouraging words. Reggie Petry, a friend and brother
that showed me the true meaning of getting down to the
wire. Through his skills and expertise he helped me
invaluably. He can best be described with the old
expression, "work hard for your money." I'd like to
thank Jonny S. for his experience, strength and hope.
Dee Real, a young man with a determination I can't put
into words, but his dynamic style was one of the key

notes that helped me move on. Mrs. Katherine Robertson, a lady fit for the stars, a special woman that showed me some incredible hope. She let me know, at a critical time in my life, that she believed in me. Katherine, a dear friend, also inspired my faith in God, allowing me to see that I was never alone. Tony Washington, a friend and colleague that had that drive and force to initiate new ideas. Because of this I adopted the same drive. Mrs. Faylee Simpson, a true beacon of hope that helped me even as a child and continues to help me and others through her travels, always carrying the message of hope. Robert Williams, a black gallant prince who passed on February 22, 2000, but who is still a champion and man of his times.

And last but not least, I'd like to thank a very special friend of mine from Bakersfield, California, the Reverend Ismael Kimbrough, pastor of Peoples Missionary Baptist Church. I'd like to refer to him as a soul winner for Christ. Because of his patience with me when I was struggling years ago, he enabled me to trudge on, allowing me to see that my soul deserved saving.

ABOUT THE AUTHOR

Savon was born in Bakersfield,California in 1950.

He started writing when he was seven years old. His first piece, a poem about Louis Armstrong, won him a ribbon of achievement for best poem and recital. Drugs and crime took Savon in and out of California prisons and jails for over thirty years.

In jail, Savon studied many Black authors. His prison time became a spiritual and artistic journey because his passion for learning was so intense.

Once Savon was released, he went to Compton College on a student loan and studied sociology and psychology. It was very hard because of his drug use and alcoholism, but during that time he managed to achieve another award for Black poetry. His addiction landed him in and out of prison until 1992. Then the light went on; three years later, he found recovery.

Throughout those years and throughout his addiction, Savon never relented in his desire to create. To express the pains and joys, the heartfelt sorrow, yet — always hope. A commitment undying in the life of a man. A commitment undying in the life of Savon Lindsay.